W S ABERNATHY
Rockville
8/10

THE FIRST WORLD WAR

MAJOR ISSUES IN HISTORY

Editor
C. WARREN HOLLISTER
University of California, Santa Barbara

William F. Church: *The Impact of Absolutism in France: National Experience under Richelieu, Mazarin, and Louis XIV*
Robert O. Collins: *The Partition of Africa: Illusion or Necessity*
J. B. Conacher: *The Emergence of Parliamentary Democracy in Britain in the Nineteenth Century*
Gerald D. Feldman: *German War Aims, 1914-1918: The Development of an Historical Debate*
Frank J. Frost: *Democracy and the Athenians*
Paul Hauben: *The Spanish Inquisition*
Bennett D. Hill: *Church and State in the Middle Ages*
Boyd H. Hill: *The Rise of the First Reich: Germany in the Tenth Century*
C. Warren Hollister: *The Impact of the Norman Conquest*
C. Warren Hollister: *The Twelfth-Century Renaissance*
Thomas M. Jones: *The Becket Controversy*
Tom B. Jones: *The Sumerian Problem*
Jeffry Kaplow: *France on the Eve of Revolution*
Archibald Lewis: *Islamic World and the West*
Anthony Molho: *Social and Economic Foundations of the Italian Renaissance*
E. W. Monter: *European Witchcraft*
Donald Queller: *The Latin Conquest of Constantinople*
Joachim Remak: *The First World War: Causes, Conduct, Consequences*
Jeffrey Russell: *Medieval Religious Dissent*
Max Salvadori: *European Liberalism*
Arthur J. Slavin: *Humanism, Reform, and Reformation*
W. Warren Wagar: *The Idea of Progress Since the Renaissance*
Bertie Wilkinson: *The Creation of the Medieval Parliament*
L. Pearce Williams: *Relativity Theory: Its Origins and Impact on Modern Thought*
Roger L. Williams: *The Commune of Paris, 1871*

THE FIRST WORLD WAR:

Causes, Conduct, Consequences

EDITED BY

Joachim Remak

John Wiley & Sons, Inc.

New York · London · Sydney · Toronto

Library of Congress Catalogue Card Number 70-142719

Cloth: ISBN 0-471-71634-0 Paper: ISBN 0-471-71635-9

Printed in the United States of America

10 9 8 7 6 5 4 3 2 1

SERIES PREFACE

The reading program in a history survey course traditionally has consisted of a large two-volume textbook and, perhaps, a book of readings. This simple reading program requires few decisions and little imagination on the instructor's part, and tends to encourage in the student the virtue of careful memorization. Such programs are by no means things of the past, but they certainly do not represent the wave of the future.

The reading program in survey courses at many colleges and universities today is far more complex. At the risk of over-simplification, and allowing for many exceptions and overlaps, it can be divided into four categories: (1) textbook, (2) original source readings, (3) specialized historical essays and interpretive studies, and (4) historical problems.

After obtaining an overview of the course subject matter (textbook), sampling the original sources, and being exposed to selective examples of excellent modern historical writing (historical essays), the student can turn to the crucial task of weighing various possible interpretations of major historical issues. It is at this point that memory gives way to creative critical thought. The "problems approach," in other words, is the intellectual climax of a thoughtfully conceived reading program and is, indeed, the most characteristic of all approaches to historical pedagogy among the newer generation of college and university teachers.

The historical problems books currently available are many and varied. Why add to this information explosion? Because the Wiley Major Issues Series constitutes an endeavor to produce something new that will respond to pedagogical needs thus far unmet. First, it is a series of individual volumes—one per problem. Many good teachers would much prefer to select their own historical issues rather than be tied to an inflexible sequence of issues imposed by a publisher and bound together between two covers. Second, the Wiley Major Issues Series is based on the idea of approaching the significant problems of history through a deft interweaving of primary sources and secondary analysis, fused together by the skill of a scholar-editor. It is felt that the essence of a historical issue cannot be satisfactorily probed either by placing a body of undigested source materials into the hands of inexperienced students or by limiting these students to the controversial literature of modern scholars who debate the meaning of sources the student never sees. This series approaches historical problems by exposing students to both the finest historical thinking on the issue and some of the evidence on which this thinking is based. This synthetic approach should prove far more fruitful than either the raw-source approach or the exclusively second-hand approach, for it combines the advantages—and avoids the serious disadvantages—of both.

Finally, the editors of the individual volumes in the Major Issues Series have been chosen from among the ablest scholars in their fields. Rather than faceless referees, they are historians who know their issues from the inside and, in most instances, have themselves contributed significantly to the relevant scholarly literature. It has been the editorial policy of this series to permit the editor-scholars of the individual volumes the widest possible latitude both in formulating their topics and in organizing their materials. Their scholarly competence has been unquestioningly respected; they have been encouraged to approach the problems as they see fit. The titles and themes of the series volumes have been suggested in nearly every case by the scholar-editors themselves. The criteria have been (1) that the issue be of relevance to undergraduate lecture courses in history, and (2) that it be an issue which the scholar-editor knows thoroughly and in which he has done creative work. And, in general, the second criterion has been given precedence over the first. In short, the question "What are the significant historical issues today?" has been answered not by general editors or sales departments but by the scholar-teachers who are responsible for these volumes.

University of California,
Santa Barbara

C. Warren Hollister

Europe . . . is inhabited by nations that sing before they kill each other.

The French and the Germans will soon be singing.

GEORGES SOREL, December 1912

INTRODUCTION

Some major problems of the early twentieth century have continued unchanged into its later part. People, in 1914, were very good at deploring war, and not nearly as good at preventing it. They also, once a war that few had planned and none had wanted (certainly not in the form it took) was underway, were not very effective at controlling it, so that in the end ten million were dead, though for decades to come there would be much argument, between nation and nation, and within each nation as well, on just why they had had to die. It definitely was not for the effects the war had, since a great majority of these—the Bolshevization of Russia, for instance, or the destruction of two empires and the critical weakening of a third, or the decline in European power in the world—had been far from the minds of any of the belligerents in 1914.

This book will give no universal answer on how war come about, for that evades us, but it will see how one war, the most destructive and terrifying in centuries, did. It will examine, too, what course it took, and what consequences it had, both immediate and long range. And throughout, either implicitly or explicitly, it will consider the relation between the desires of the powers that fought it, and their actions, for surely one of the great lessons of the First World War was to show again the discrepancy that exists in human history between intention and achievement, between the wish and the fact.

The book will tell its story by first letting historians and then witnesses to the events speak. The historians quoted will try for some overall views, and for objectivity; the witnesses will be more openly partisan, though there is much advantage in listening to someone who saw and heard and hurt, yet from whom, as a British nineteenth century historian put it, "the future was concealed." Neither historians nor witnesses will always agree with each other, which is one more indication of why general rules about such grand topics as war and peace are less credible than the laws of physics or even of economic life.

Still, we can learn.

JOACHIM REMAK

CONTENTS

INTRODUCTION ix

PROLOGUE 1

PART ONE

The Causes

I. HISTORIANS

1. Laurence Lafore—*Historians and Guilt Complexes* 7
2. Joachim Remak—*1914, The Third Balkan War—Origins Reconsidered* 11

II. WITNESSES

3. Gavrilo Princip 25
4. Dragutin Dimitrijević, Called Apis 26
5. Johannes Urzidil 29
6. Sergei Sazonov 31
7. Alphonse Grasset 32

PART TWO

The War

III. HISTORIANS

8. Bernadotte E. Schmitt—*The First World War, 1914–1918* 37
9. George F. Kennan—*The Price We Paid for War* 46

IV. WITNESSES

10. Raymond Jubert 51
11. Ernst Jünger 53
12. Manfred von Richthofen 55
13. Sir John Monash 56
14. Sir Arthur Conan Doyle 57

15. W. H. L. Watson 59
16. Paul von Hindenburg 61
17. Lord Bryce 63
18. Alphonse Grasset 67
19. Gerald Brenan 68
20. Ljubomir Dabić 70
21. Ferdinand Foch 74

PART THREE

The Consequences

V. HISTORIANS

22. A. J. P. Taylor—*Afterwards—1919* 77
23. René Albrecht Carrié—*Economic Consequences* 81
24. Raymond J. Sontag—*Between the Wars* 86
25. Gordon A. Craig—*The Revolution in War and Diplomacy* 92

VI. WITNESSES

26. John Reed 105
27. Harold Nicolson 109
28. Adolf Hitler 111

EPILOGUE

Note on Further Reading 117

THE FIRST WORLD WAR

PROLOGUE

Actually, this picture of a golden age, of an ordered, stable, and pacific Europe, was deceptive. In greater or less degree, social unrest was widespread, and growing more and more active.

BERNADOTTE SCHMITT

I do not envy yr. gadgets. I'd be ready to forgo them all including telephones, electricity, autos if only I could recapture *la douceur de vivre* of the years before 1914.

BERNARD BERENSON to PETER VIERECK

. . . "By the opening years of this century you were born in," he said, . . . "the citizens of Christendom proudly stood on a pinnacle of material power that exceeded every previous dream of man. Moreover, the pinnacle had been built by man's own efforts and hence invited an understandable pride. It had been built by human reason, by "the scientific method," by a rapidly growing technology. The rules were already known by which this mighty skyscraper city could be built even higher. To the critic who scoffed that it was a purely material achievement, modern man could reply that not only were he and his fellow citizens more comfortable physically than their fathers had been but that liberalism was everywhere triumphant or about to triumph, that political privilege had been sharply curtailed, that economic privilege was under attack, that, in short, social justice was a goal universally professed. If religion and art seemed often to be lagging, might not that be that they still lacked an adequate material base? Seek ye first a high standard of living, and all these things shall

SOURCE. Stringfellow Barr, *Purely Academic* (New York: Simon & Shuster, Inc., 1958), pp. 158–159. Reprinted by permission of the author.

be added unto you. It was good to be alive in the years of man's unbelievable power and of man's increasing hope for the future. It was good to be alive in the opening years of the twentieth century, this century, your century and mine, for they were in all truth wonderful, glittering years."

He paused and looked about him as if in sudden pain. Some of his students stared curiously. Breathing harder, he began again.

"From this bourgeois, Baconian Eden modern man was ejected with a sudden violence unique in his experience. In a few days, millions of men were mobilized to kill and be killed. It was as if some terrible madness had seized on the citizens of the city that Matter and Force had so benignly ruled. Across the tranquil, smiling, midsummer countryside of Europe swept vast armies, bearing more deadly weapons than man had ever known. The earth rocked and the sky reeled. The great gray ships of the British Royal Navy hurried silently to their appointed posts. It was the summer of 1914."

Suddenly, such violent emotions arose in Schneider that he knew he could not go on. He glanced at his watch. There was lots of time left—but it was time he could not use. His throat became dry; his voice came to his own ears as if from a great distance. He felt slightly dizzy.

"I cannot discuss the First World War today. I am sorry." . . .

PART ONE
The Causes

Despite the state of tension between the Triple Alliance and the Triple Entente, and whatever may have been the ambitions or the aspirations, the grievances or the anxieties of nations and governments, it was not inevitable that general war should break out in the summer of 1914.

But, fully aware of the unpreparedness of Russia, France and England, William II had renounced the peaceful attitude he had taken during the recent Balkan Wars . . . He and the German general staff were in a mood for aggression. They decided to use the first favorable opportunity to adopt a policy of force. And Vienna, encouraged by Berlin, was inclined toward an attack on Serbia, at the risk of provoking the European complications that might follow upon Russia's resistance to any disturbance of the *status quo* in the Balkans. . . .

CAMILLE BLOCH, *Les causes de la guerre mondiale*

Germany pursued no aim either in Europe or elsewhere that could only be achieved by means of war.

Austria-Hungary's only aim was to maintain the *status quo*. Her initial intention of rectifying her borders at Serbia's expense was immediately abandoned at Germany's insistence, and even Sazonov was convinced of her disinterest in territorial acquisitions by her definite statements.

France aimed at recovering Alsace-Lorraine, and many leading French politicians also hoped to annex the Saar basin, while Russia aspired to possession of Constantinople and the Straits. Both powers knew well that these aims could not be achieved without a European war. . . .

GRAF MAX VON MONTGELAS, *Leitfaden zur Kriegsschuldfrage*

My father gave me the poems of Georg Trakl for my birthday.

Franz Kafka told me that Trakl had committed suicide by poison, to escape the horrors of the war.

"Desertion into death," I said.

"He had too much imagination," said Kafka. "That is why he could not stand the war, which above all else was caused by a tremendous lack of imagination."

GUSTAV JANOUCH, *Conversations with Kafka*

I HISTORIANS

The basic facts about the origins of the First World War seem simple enough. On June 28, 1914, seven assassins wait for the heir to the throne of Austria-Hungary, Archduke Franz Ferdinand. The scene is Sarajevo, capital of Bosnia-Herzegovina, a region recently annexed by Austria, but contested by Serbia, which would like to join the ethnically largely South Slav territory to its own, to form a Greater Serbia. One of the assassins throws a bomb, and misses. Another fires his pistol, and kills both the archduke and his wife.

The Austrians, suspecting, though they have no proof, that there must be some links between the assassins and Belgrade, decide to crush Serbia. On July 28, after first presenting Serbia with an ultimatum that is meant to be rejected, they declare war on that country.

What has begun as a local conflict between Austria and Serbia quickly spreads. The Austrians, before deciding on war, had assured themselves of the unconditional support of their German ally. The Germans, for a variety of reasons—among which the desire for a spectacular diplomatic success, and the fear of losing Austria as an ally were the most obvious—have given Vienna the desired blank check. The Serbians, for their part, now turn for assistance to their principal ally, Russia. The Russians, again for a variety of reasons that strike *them* as sound—among them the desire for a diplomatic success, and the fear of losing Serbia as an ally—on July 29 mobilize their troops along their borders with both Germany and Austria. Thereupon the Germans, having made a fruitless attempt to get the Tzar to rescind the mobilization orders, declare war against Russia on August 1. To this they add, two days later, a declaration of war against Russia's Western ally, France. The Germans's calculation is that France would enter the war in any case, and that their only chance to win a two front war against both France and Russia was to strike very quickly. Thus they not only declare war on France as well as on Russia, but on August 3 invade Belgium, in order to circumvent some of the main French defenses. This action —which implements the famous Schlieffen Plan, first worked out by the German general staff nearly a decade before 1914—brings Great Britain into the war. England, though loosely allied with France, might well have remained neutral had it not been for the violation of Belgium's neutrality, and the German threat to the channel ports.

Thus, by early August 1914, the members of Europe's two great alliance systems are, with one exception, at war with each other. The exception is Italy, nominally a member of the Triple Alliance with Germany and Austria. But aside from that, the Central Powers of Germany and Austria now face the Triple Entente of Russia, France, and Great Britain in battle.

That same year, Turkey joins the Central Powers. A year later, Bulgaria does. The Triple Entente is to find even more allies. Within the next three years, it is joined by eighteen other powers. The most important among them are Japan, which enters the war on the Allied side in 1914, Italy (1915), and the United States (1917). The Austro-Serbian war has become a European war, the European war a World War.

This outline of events clearly is a very much simplified one. Beyond these bare facts there is a mass of details, nearly all of which lend themselves to radically different interpretations. Who was the aggressor in the East, Germany or Russia? What, if any, advance knowledge did the Serbian government possess about Sarajevo? How well did various individual diplomats and politicians manage affairs during the crisis of July and August 1914? Multitudes of questions, multitudes of answers. A host of answers, too, on the matter of the larger, underlying causes of the war. Could the clash between Serbia and Austria, between modern, dynamic nationalism and the older, static concept of a multinational, multiracial state possibly have been avoided? Was there a will to war in the Europe of 1914? Or was there too much innocence? To what extent was the alliance system to blame? And what was the responsibility of each of the countries involved? It was on this last issue, and particularly on the question of the degree of Germany's culpability, that much of the debate, scholarly and otherwise, centered in the years that immediately followed the war, as it has again recently. The passage that follows indicates the reasons for that approach, as well as its limits.

1 FROM *Laurence Lafore* *Historians and Guilt Complexes*

Lafore (b. 1917) is a novelist as well as a historian of distinction, who has taught at Swarthmore, and now is at the University of Iowa. The Long Fuse *is one of the best and most balanced accounts of the causes of 1914. Not the least of the book's virtues is that it directs our attention again to the essentially Southeast European origins of 1914 reminding us that "the war, that vast phenomenon, grew out of a single international event, which was the conflict between the Habsburg Monarchy and the kingdom of Serbia. Had Austria-Hungary been differently constituted, had Serbia posed a less lethal threat to it, there would have been no Austro-Serbian war in 1914; and if a general war had come later, it would have been fought on different terms and taken different forms."*

Until the moment when German troops crossed the Belgian border and entered the frontier villages on the early morning of August 4, 1914, the conduct of the affairs of state that led to the invasion had been in the hands of diplomats, politicians, and military advisers. At that moment the events of the recent past were transferred to the hands of others, of publicists and propagandists. For four years an unconscionable volume of self-defense and corresponding vilification was poured forth. None of it was accurate, let alone complete. Official publications—the *British Blue Book*, the *French Yellow Book*, the *German White Book*, the *Austrian Red Book*, the *Russian Orange Book*—sought to demonstrate, by a judicious selection from the archives, the moral purity of each nation and its allies and the depravity of the enemy. The selections were by necessity small, and by reason of their purpose highly misleading. Judicious omissions were sometimes supplemented by falsification. Legends were accepted in the belief that the end of victory for the democratic nations justified an incautious credulity for rumors.

The belief was sound. For every nation the necessary sacrifices imposed by war had to be justified by belief in the guilt of the enemy

SOURCE. Laurence Lafore, *The Long Fuse: An Interpretation of the Origins of World War I* (New York: J.B. Lippincott Company, 1965), pp. 18–22. Reprinted by permission of the publisher.

for starting it, and the necessary energy had to be ignited by enthusiasm and hatred. There is no doubt that this was true; modern wars are fought largely by emotion and by the creative forces that emotion, properly directed, can release; and the degree of emotion required in an age of literate publics and industrial economics was proportionately greater than ever before. Where the conviction of the public about the righteousness of its cause faltered, as it did in Russia, the nation at war collapsed into an appalling tangle of distraught individuals. The leaders elsewhere, whose moral and legal obligation was to prevent precisely such a calamity, were shrewd and skillful enough to promote the calling forth of hatred. The public response was gratifying.

When the peace treaty was at length written, it became expedient for quite accidental reasons to include in it, in passing, the statement that "the Allied and Associated Governments affirm and Germany accepts the responsibility of Germany and her allies for causing all the loss and damage to which the Allied and Associated Governments and their nationals have been subjected as a consequence of the war imposed upon them by the aggression of Germany and her allies." So thoroughly had the opinion among the Allied and Associated governments been convinced of the responsibility of Germany and Austria-Hungary for deliberately starting the first World War that the statement passed almost unnoticed in Britain, France, and the United States. But in Germany, where precisely the opposite view of the origins of the war had been implanted and received with precisely the same degree of passionate acceptance, the passage was regarded not only as wholly untrue—intolerably insulting—but as further evidence of the ineffable hypocrisy of the enemy states. The discussion of moral guilt for starting the war, instead of fading away when the war ended, was renewed with greater intensity than ever. Instead of being fought by publicists, the battle of "war guilt" now became the concern of whole armies of historians. The flow of literature was torrential. No historical subjects except the American Civil War and the French Revolution had ever been examined with this exhausting thoroughness. The unprecedented volume of primary sources was supplemented by learned monographs. Regular periodicals devoted to the causes of the war were established, and flourished. Day-by-day accounts of the crisis were followed by hour-by-hour and, literally, minute-by-minute accounts. It was clear, for example, that the sequence of receipt and dispatch of diplomatic telegrams was very important, and there were erudite articles computing the time required in different capitals for decoding.

An interesting development began to take place in the mid-1920's. In all of the erstwhile belligerent countries, and most noticeably in Britain and America, there was a contagion of breast-beating. What was called "revisionism," one of whose forebears was a sullen economic expert on the British delegation at the Peace Conference named John Maynard Keynes who dramatized both the economic and the moral defects of Allied policies, became popular. Moved by embarrassment at the hysterical excesses of wartime propoganda, and faced with what seemed incontrovertible evidence in the impressively edited collections of German documents that the German Republic was bringing out, British and American historians discovered that the Germans had certainly not been guilty of *planning* a world war and that the conduct of the Russian, the French, and even the British governments conspicuously failed to demonstrate any single-minded devotion to the preservation of peace.

Then the approach of a second World War, and the startling evolution of a new Germany that was not only openly but boastfully aggressive, caused a species of counterrevisionism to emerge. Historians began to apprehend everywhere that there was something deep and rooted in the German people and the German state that led them to undertake wars of aggression.

The river of literature subsided. There were now more immediate subjects of interest, and it seemed that almost all that could be said about 1914 had been said. From the mid-thirties on, there was a rapid decline in writings about 1914.

But the river did not dry up completely. There appeared, a few years after the end of the war, the immense and imposing work of Luigi Albertini, by all odds the most compendious, reliable, and closely reasoned of all treatments. Albertini had not merely studied the documents and memoirs—studied more of them, since more were available—than had earlier scholars. He had also interviewed many of the statesmen, starting in 1919, and had asked them embarrassing questions to which honest answers were difficult to avoid, since, like a masterly prosecuting attorney, Albertini had skill and knowledge that made cross-examination easy and lethal.

The trend of Albertini's conclusions was to some extent in the fashion of the times: he found the Germans unquestionably guilty.

Not by any means solely guilty, not guilty of planning a world war years in advance, but unquestionably guilty of urging Austria to attack Serbia at the known risk of a general war.

This interpretation of 1914 is now generally held among those who write about it. Indeed, the reinculpation of Germany has since been carried much farther than it was by Albertini. On the fortieth anniversary of the crisis, for example, the Regius Professor of History at Oxford published in *The New York Times Magazine* a commemorative article in which he said that it had been finally and definitely "proved that the War was caused by deliberate German aggression." The single fact produced in support of this assertion by Professor Trevor-Roper would not seem final or definite to a close student of the chronology of events, but his attitude is nonetheless illuminating. Six years later, the distinguished German historian Fritz Fischer published a history of German policy before and during the war called *Griff nach der Weltmacht*. In it he said that he was not concerned with the allocation of guilt; still, he allocated it, concluding that the German leaders "bear an important portion of the responsibility" for the European war. In demonstration of this, he produced new evidence of a damning sort, and argued with considerable force that a policy of willingness to embark on preventive war had been decided before the crisis, based on a wildly optimistic appraisal of German chances for victory. Austria-Hungary, he said, was to a large extent pushed into war at German insistence. His book occasioned much discussion and some shock in Gemany.

Professor Fischer's treatment of the crisis is brief; most of his materials have been used before and subjected to different interpretations. Anyone who has read his account must admit that the Germans were, at least, frivolously willing to contemplate the possibility of a "preventive war" and were exploiting the occasion for a "grab at world power"; still, his treatment is very narrowly of the German side of things, and a wider survey indicates clearly that the Germans were by no means the only people who were prepared to risk a war and who had expansionist programs in their minds. Russians were also ready to grasp at world power. And the fact remains that it was the crisis of Austro-Serb relations that brought these and other ambitions and alarms into open conflict. The question of the guilt of individuals and nations dissolves, as Fischer admits, into an ocean of general responsibility.

2 FROM *Joachim Remak* *1914, The Third Balkan War—Origins Reconsidered*

Yet the ocean can be traversed. One way of doing so is to use Fischer's approach, and to see what each power, not Germany alone, was bidding for in 1914. The following paper, after examining the various general factors that are sometimes held responsible for the war—economic and imperialist rivalries, for instance, or the roles played by militarism, by the press and public opinion, and by the European alliance system—and finding that none of them, by themselves, were sufficient to cause a war, continues:

. . . We are back with the inescapable question of the responsibility of men and nations. It is just as well. For there was nothing that new about the international mood of 1914. Alliances have always been with us, and so has the volatility of public opinion. Statesmen and nations have forever had to operate in an atmosphere of potential violence. The question that matters is how well each nation managed its affairs in the actual world in which it found itself in 1914, and not in an ideal one of no entangling alliances, of colonial satiety, of the rule of world law, or of a press that promoted nothing but brotherhood. Let us then, in this spirit, consider the responsibility of each of the belligerents in ascending order.

FRANCE AND BRITAIN

The nation that can be held least responsible for the outbreak of the war is France. This is so even if we bear in mind all the revisions of historical judgments, and all the revisions of these revisions, to which we have now been treated. And it is so even if we use Fischer's approach, and ask ourselves just what the aims of France were, in the years that preceded war and after. Now it is true that some of the

SOURCE. Joachim Remak, "1914, The Third Balkan War—Origins Reconsidered," paper presented at the Second Congress of Southeast European Studies at Athens, May 1970. This will be the only selection from that author.

things that some of the French were making a bid for entailed the risk of war. More than a generation after Frankfurt,[1] a majority of Frenchmen still had not reconciled themselves to the loss of Alsace and Lorraine. Poincaré and his friends were still pursuing what Boulanger had, except that they were doing so with greater intelligence, patience, tact, and skill and, hence, with greater effectiveness. The desire to undo the decision of Frankfurt was as powerful a motive force in France's system of alliances as any. Germany, to put the matter differently, did not wish for any territorial change in Europe between 1871 and 1914; France did. It was equally true that during the July crisis, France failed to urge restraint on St. Petersburg. One cannot very well indict the Germans for their blank check to Austria without noting that the Russians held a similar piece of paper from France.

Yet how tentative and cautious the bid to recover the lost provinces was. When we consider the restraints that the French were imposing upon themselves in the pursuit of their aims, how minor the responsibility of France must appear. The French might mourn Strasbourg, but they were plotting no war to retake it. Even the most irreconcilable groups of Frenchmen were organizing no Pan-Gallic movements; there was nothing in France to compare, for ambition and folly, with either the Pan-Slavs or the Pan-Germans. Also, all speculations about France's ultimate objectives have about them a certain irrelevancy. Perhaps France would, some day, have fought to avenge Sedan, perhaps France would not. We will never know. The fact is that the French, in August 1914, did not go to war for Alsace, but because the Germans, lacking the political imagination and the diplomatic skill to keep France neutral, first presented an unacceptable ultimatum and then began to march on Paris.

The French, in 1914, entered the war because they had no alternative. The Germans had attacked them. History can be very simple at times.

But if the French had no choice once the Schlieffen Plan had gone into effect, the British did. (The British public certainly thought so, and so did several members of the government.) What then was Britain bidding for in 1914? That question seems to matter more today than the point discussed at such length in the twenties and thirties of whether the British had given sufficient notice of their intent to protect Belgium to the Germans. That whole argument—and it includes the implication that if only the British caveat had been stronger, the

[1] The victor's peace that ended the Franco-Prussian war of 1870–1871.

Germans might have acted with greater restraint—strikes us as fairly unreal today. For no matter what Grey's[2] precise words, or what his silences, any responsible German statesman must have known that it was a matter of vital interest to Great Britain whether France survived as a power, and who would control the channel ports of Belgium and France. . . .

No, let us consider the British bid instead. What was involved here was no sudden, novel move, but something quite long-range. There had taken place, in the half-century or so before the war, a tremendous expansion of British power, accompanied by a pronounced lack of sympathy for any similar ambitions on the part of other nations. If any nation was compensation-conscious, it was Great Britain; if the Austrians wished to occupy Bosnia, for instance, then the British must have Cyprus. Even without this particular diplomatic gambit, the British, between the eighteen-seventies and the turn of the century, were adding, adding, adding to their Empire: Burma, Egypt, Uganda, Somaliland, Kenya, Zanzibar, Rhodesia, the Boer Republic, all were flying the Union Jack. If any nation had truly made a bid for world power, it was Great Britain. In fact, it had more than bid for it. It had achieved it. The Germans were merely talking about building a railway to Baghdad. The Queen of England *was* Empress of India. If any nation had upset the world's balance of power, it was Great Britain.

The usually more modest appetites of others, however, were a different matter. That the French in Morocco or the Germans in South West Africa were doing quite as well as colonizers as were the British in Uganda was something that seemed very difficult to perceive through the London fog. British territorial acquisitions were a part of the progress of mankind; those of others were a menace to world peace and civilization. Russia's desire for access to the Mediterranean was a provocation; Britannia Rule the Waves reflected a noble and natural sentiment.

After the turn of the century, this attitude was directed with special force at Germany, although it was seldom made clear just what the Germans were to do with all *their* excess energy. Some of the British documents of the period convey an impression of near-hysteria in the face of a rising Germany, reaching from a British admiral's simple suggestion to sink the German fleet without warning, to the more erudite memoranda of some of the senior officials of the foreign office

[2] Sir Edward Grey, British foreign secretary 1905–1916.

decrying the German menace. Unfortunately, if one nation imagines for long enough that another is "the natural enemy," as a much circulated foreign office memorandum had it, the likelihood is strong that the other nation will some day have to play the role it has been assigned.

That judgment does not exculpate the Germans, who had been willing to endorse a Balkan war that clearly contained the risk of a war in the West. As far as Great Britain's direct responsibility for the final crisis and the outbreak of hostilities is concerned, it is indisputably less than Germany's. It was units of the German army, not of the British navy, who were sending shells into Belgium. Before the guns had been moved into position, however, it can scarcely be said that the British did much better in restraining the Eastern member of the Triple Entente than they would accuse the Germans of doing vis-à-vis Vienna. "Will to war" is too grand and at the same time elusive a term to use with any degree of comfort, but what do we do about the memory of what would happen a quarter of a century later? In 1938, when the British definitely did not wish war, their prime minister would hurry to Germany three times within the space of two weeks and negotiate peace under terms far worse than those of 1914 with a leader infinitely more dangerous than the Kaiser in his most Wagnerian moods. The lamps were not "going out" (Lord Grey's celebrated figure of speech) in 1914. Many people, the author of the phrase included, were helping to put them out.

RUSSIA AND GERMANY

What, though, of Russia's will to war, or rather of the willingness to accept war as a possible means of policy? Here, too, our emphasis today may profitably be shifted away from some earlier assumptions. The Russian response to the Austrian threat against Serbia, as we know, consisted not only of mobilization against Austria, but against Germany as well. Here, the argument went, was Russia's major responsibility for the war. She was the first great power to mobilize. Not only that, but the manner of her mobilization frustrated all hopes for localizing the conflict; what could the Germans do but react with military means. And above all, the Russian decision came at a time when mobilization was understood to equal war.

Today, the argument seems only partly valid. For mobilization did not automatically have to mean war—except to the Germans, that is, for whom each minute counted lest the Schlieffen Plan was to fail. For every other nation, peaceful alternatives existed even after the men had been called to arms.

Not that the old argument was wholly irrelevant. For the Tsar and his advisers, by their behavior at the end of July, indicated very plainly that they were perfectly well aware that mobilization, while not war, was more than a symbolic show of strength, and was bound to be interpreted as an act of war by Germany. Then why did they go ahead with it? Because, and here we owe much to Fischer again and his approach of looking at a nation's boldest dreams, it was a question of the whole thrust of Russia's foreign policy over the decades that preceded Sarajevo. 1914 was not the first time that Russia refused to rule out the possibility of war in the pursuit of certain long-range aims. Since the middle of the nineteenth century, Russia had been involved directly in two wars—the Crimean War and the War of 1877–1878—indirectly in two more—the Balkan Wars of 1912 and 1913—and, directly or indirectly, in crises too numerous to list, all with the intent of weakening the empire of the Sultan to the benefit of that of the Tsar. It was a policy that acted as an irritant to Austro-Russian relations; threats to one's survival tend to annoy. Yet the Russians persisted. It was Russia rather than Austria that was the expansionist power in Southeastern Europe. The Annexation Crisis[3] was the exception, not the rule. Under ordinary circumstances, Austria had considerably more to fear from Russia's Balkan ambitions than Russia had from Austria's, even if we add the reservation that customarily, Russian official policy was more restrained and rational than some of the truly extravagant Pan-Slav spokesmen would have liked. Customarily, for in July 1914, as it had on some previous occasions, the borderline between Pan-Slavism and government policy once more became blurred. If Serbia chose to resist Austria's demands, then Russia would support its Slavic brethren. The story of Germany's "blank check" to Austria is well known, but the Russians were doing no better at counseling caution on Belgrade. On the contrary, St. Petersburg was giving Serbia as much reason to rely on Russian support as Berlin was giving Austria to rely on that of Germany.

Perhaps the Russians had no real choice. Caution would have

[3] The crisis caused by Austria's annexation of Bosnia and Herzegovina in 1908. One reason for the gravity of the crisis was that Serbia, with some encouragement from Russia, felt that it had a strong ethnic claim to the formerly Turkish-held area.

equalled surrender, and 1908 was too recent a memory. This time, the alternative to active military aid might indeed have been a grave diminution of Russian influence not only in Serbia but throughout the Balkans. Certainly the Austrians had had no reason to assume that Russia would merely look on, let alone look the other way, while they were shooting their way into Belgrade. Though if we say that, must we not in fairness add that the Russians had no more right to expect the Germans to acquiesce in a Habsburg fiasco?

Here it is, the question of German guilt. How do we deal with it, after Fischer? We deal with it in large part as non-revisionist historians have before, by simply saying that German responsibility for 1914 goes back at least to the 1890's, to the whole conduct of German diplomacy after Bismarck. The master's touch was shown by moderation, the touch of his successors by what Bismarck had accused post-Cavour Italy of: a large appetite and poor teeth. And to what did Germany's appetite really run after 1890? To "world power," to rivalry with Britain, to a German Central Africa, to security against France? None of these policies had been thought through. Activity there was aplenty; what was lacking was direction. "Oh Ernest isn't silent," runs an Oscar Wilde line in *A Woman of No Importance*. "He talks the whole time. But he has got no conversation."

By 1914, as a result of the Kaiser's and his friends' talking all the while, a new specter had come to haunt Europe, the specter of *furor teutonicus*. German behavior in the final crisis certainly did little to banish it. The list of German blunders is an all too familiar one: the blank check to Austria; the failure, once it had become plain that an Austro-Serbian war was likely to become European in scope, to search for a compromise with every last ounce of energy; the final triumph of the military over the political rationale with the invasion of Belgium and France. "During the whole crisis prior to August 4, 1914," writes a historian whose sympathies are anything but anti-German, "not a single constructive move was made by Germany to stave off the impending disaster."[4]

The list is familiar, so familiar that we need to pause, and see if there is no another side to it. Just what were Germany's motives in 1914? Was it really a bid for world power that impelled the Germans to invite disaster?

Actually, Germany's motives were far less sinister than this, though

[4] Hajo Holborn, *A History of Modern Germany, 1840–1945* (New York, 1969), p. 427.

that makes them no more wise. Motives, of course, are seldom unambiguous or simple, but two great desires seem to dominate Germany's actions. One was to maintain the Austrian alliance. The other was to use the Sarajevo crisis to register a spectacular diplomatic victory, to break what Berlin considered the noose of Allied encirclement. As for the defense of Austria, it was not only that the Germans were afraid, as has been said often enough, of losing their last ally. It was also that they feared that if Austria failed to cope with the crisis posed by Franz Ferdinand's assassination, the country would be finished as a great power. "We must maintain Austria proper," was the way Bethmann Hollweg[5] put it in the summer of 1914. "Were Russia to unleash the South Slavs, we would be lost."[6] As for the concurrent diplomatic coup, the Germans felt, and rightly so, that their luck was running out, that their prestige had seldom been lower, and that they faced an overwhelmingly hostile Europe. A show of strength—and on an issue where moral right appeared to be on their side, as it did after Sarajevo—might radically alter that situation. To quote the German Chancellor again: if the gamble should succeed, "if war does not break out, if the Tsar is unwilling or France, alarmed, counsels peace, we have the prospect of splitting the Entente."[7]

Too many if's, we know. And besides, the German gamble was based on two major miscalculations. One was that Austria would act quickly, would move "immediately in the wake of the murder." There would thus be "a rapid *fait accompli*, and afterwards friendship toward the Entente."[8] The other was that the worst risk the Germans were able to imagine was that of a limited, local war.

It was these two miscalculations that account for Germany's fearful part of the responsibility. These and the Schlieffen Plan of course, which inevitably spread the war once the Austrians had made their leisurely move against Serbia, and the Russians would not be deterred from coming to that country's aid. And as the gamble started to go wrong, the diplomats found that there was no way to withdraw their stakes. What had begun as a diplomatic move (admittedly a risky

[5] Theobald von Bethmann Hollweg. German Chancellor 1909–1917.

[6] Bethmann to Riezler, July 20, 1914. Konrad H. Jarausch, "The Illusion of Limited War: Chancellor Bethmann Hollweg's Calculated Risk, July 1914," *Central European History*, II, No. 1 (March 1969), p. 62. Jarausch's article probably is the most important single contribution to the whole recent debate on Germany's responsibility.

[7] Bethmann to Riezler, July 8, 1914, *ibid.*, p. 58.

[8] Riezler diary, *ibid.*, pp. 60 and 68.

one) had passed, in the nature of things, into the hands of the generals. "We have lost control and the landslide has begun."[9]

It is here that Germany's guilt lies, not in dreams of world domination. It lies, to repeat it, in risks taken that were immeasurably too high; in allowing military planners to dictate policy; and beyond that, in the general amateurishness that marked the nation's diplomatic behavior in the quarter century before Sarajevo. These things were quite bad enough. There is no need to add imaginary sins to real ones.

AUSTRIA, SOME BOSNIANS, AND SERBIA

But how had the Germans become involved in the first place? Through a minor and obscure Balkan quarrel? Yes, if by obscure we mean that it was insufficiently understood by outsiders, and by minor that no vital interests of the great powers were involved. To the two nations directly affected, however, to Austria and Serbia, few crises could have mattered more, or been clearer in their implications, than Sarajevo. And both nations behaved with great recklessness in 1914.

We have stood stooped over for too long now, searching for the underlying causes of the war. We have become so involved in subtleties that the obvious has sometimes escaped us; we have not seen the forest for the roots. The obvious fact is that the issue that led to Verdun and Versailles not only was Austro-Serb in origin but that in the immediate crisis that followed, some of the most basic decisions affecting peace or war were made by Berchtold rather than Bethmann, and by Pašić rather than Sazonov.[10]

It is a moot question which nation practiced the worse sort of brinkmanship. Let us evade it by dealing with them in alphabetical order. As for Austria, then, it was the whole general direction of the Ballplatz's policy after Sarajevo, and the ultimatum of July 23 in particular, that invited war with Serbia, and general war as well.[11] What an appalling document it was—tardy, incompetent, deceptive,

[9] Bethmann to Riezler, July 30, 1914. *ibid.*, p. 69.

[10] Berchtold was foreign minister of Austria-Hungry in 1914, Pašić was Serbia's prime minister, and Sazonov foreign minister of Russia.

[11] Later theories that Berchtold acted as he did only because he never really meant to come close to the brink, since in his secret soul he felt confident that the Germans would before long restrain him, are just that—theories. See A. J. P. Taylor, *War by Time-Table, How the First World War Began* (London, 1969), pp. 62 and 65–66.

designed to be rejected. Austria was setting the course, and neither friend nor foe had been allowed an honest look at its direction.

It is entirely possible, of course, to present a case for the defense. Sarajevo was no pretense; the Habsburg monarchy had some perfectly legitimate interests to defend—Serbia was a good deal closer to Austria than Southeast Asia is to the United States. Surely, self-preservation is as sensible and honorable a motive as any, and the state one wished to maintain had a great deal to be said in its favor. "My whole libido," wrote Dr. Freud the day after Serbia's reply had been received, "goes out to Austria-Hungary."

What alternative did the Habsburg monarchy have? Its vital interests were involved, in a way those of no other European state were in 1914; not Russia's and not Germany's, not those of France nor of Great Britain. Of all of Europe's crises and conflicts, the Austro-Serbian issue was unique in that it seemed to allow no leeway between either surrender or war. None of the others had "led to actions that produced war. They were either negotiable or repressible. The one problem that was neither negotiable nor repressible was that raised by threats to the integrity of Austria-Hungary."[12]

Still, to understand all is *not* to forgive all. It is true enough that, as a committee of distinguished French and German historians put it in 1952, "the documents do not permit attributing, to any government or nation, a premeditated desire for European war in 1914."[13] But Berchtold, and Conrad,[14] had very much of a premeditated desire for a little Balkan war, to recover some of the monarchy's lost prestige. Did they want that war to spread? No, but the truth was that the reckless and inadequate people who were deciding policy in Vienna did not really care. This was Austria's war; perhaps only the fact that the countrymen of Johann Strauss and Sigmund Freud ordinarily made such poor villains (there would be some fairly obvious exceptions such as Adolf Hitler) allowed that simple fact to be forgotten so thoroughly.

Austria's war, and Serbia's. Two Austrian victims, seven Bosnian assassins, and no one can say to this day how many Serbian helpers. Sarajevo was more than an excuse for war. It was one of its major causes.

[12] Laurence Lafore, *The Long Fuse*, p. 268.

[13] *Deutsch-französische Vereinbarung uber strittige Fragen europäischer Geschichte* (Brunswick, 1958) pp. 11 and 27.

[14] Austria's chief of staff.

The assassins, in a sense, were innocents. Had he known that his deed might mean war, one of them said during his trial, he would have preferred his own death to that of his victims. But he was speaking for himself, not for Colonel Dimitrijević.[15] Apis was a man who considered the consequences of his actions.

But to what extent did the involvement of Serbia's chief of military intelligence reflect on his government? The assassination, after all, had been planned by the Black Hand during the Colonel's off-duty hours, and not by Pašić or any of his ministers. In fact, was not the crime a largely local affair, and is not the question whether any of the assassins even belonged to the Black Hand still unresolved?

Yes and no. Of course the act had its local roots. Social ferment played its part along with national enthusiasm. The two great trends of nineteenth century Europe—nationalism, and the desire for reforms affecting the land—had not halted at the borders of Bosnia-Herzegovina. "I am from the village," said Princip at his trial. "Nine-tenths of our people are farmers who suffer," said Čabrinović,[16] "who live in misery, who have no schools, who are deprived of any culture. We sympathized with them in their distress . . . we loved our people."

Yes and no. We have complicated things too much. The roots were in Sarajevo, and they were in Belgrade. Each side was using the other. Each could do so without guilt feelings, for each loved their common nation.

Of the seven assassins, two survive to this day. One is the director of a historical institute in Belgrade, the other the curator of the ethnographic department of the Sarajevo museum. In the late sixties, this author talked to both, and two questions and answers above all others remain in his mind. Who, if any, were the Black Hand members in the group? Come now, was the answer. Perhaps some, perhaps none. What did it matter? "We have many Black Hands in this part of the world." And the question of motive? He had read all the theories, and they were all of them right, and all of them wrong. "Look, we were seventeen."

We have complicated things too much. Just what, scholars have asked for years now, did Pašić know about the preparations for Sarajevo; to what extent was the Serbian government involved? Can we trust a disgruntled minister's recollections; can we put any credence

[15] Colonel Dimitrijević, called Apis (see p. 26) was the person most involved on the Serbian side in the Sarajevo assassination.

[16] Princip's friend and fellow-assassin (see p. 25).

in some fragmentary document interpreted by an Austrian border guard? The details are complex; the experts have never been able to agree on them entirely. Yet certain basic truths really are not very complex at all. And among them is the fact that Dimitrijević's action did incriminate the Serbian government, for reasons both long-range and immediate. That government had for too many years been tolerating or even encouraging a movement for a Greater Serbia, whose aims were bound to be offensive to Austria-Hungary, and whose methods were bound to be offensive to anyone. Very specifically speaking, the government in 1914 had taken no effective action to prevent the assassination of Franz Ferdinand, of which it very probably had some foreknowledge, nor had it managed to end the influence of the Black Hand, of which it assuredly had knowledge.

Not that there was anything in the least ignoble about either Pašić's or Dimitrijević's aims. The concept of a Greater South Slav State was fully as defensible as was Austria-Hungary's right to survival. Tragedy, in the Hegelian definition, consists not of the conflict of right with wrong but of right with right. But the Serbians set about achieving their purposes with a truly frightening disregard of the consequences. Here, then, was Serbia's vast share in the responsibility for the First World War, one that was matched only by Austria's; Belgrade surely knew that it was set on collision course, yet it would not alter direction. There is, in the British files, a report from the ambassador to Vienna, Sir Fairfax Cartwright, written in January 1913 in the wake of the First Balkan War, which sums up the entire matter better than any later historian can:

"Servia will some day set Europe by the ears, and bring about a universal war on the Continent. . . . I cannot tell you how exasperated people are getting here at the continual worry which that little country causes to Austria under encouragement from Russia. It may be compared to a certain extent to the trouble we had to suffer through the hostile attitude formerly assumed against us by the Transvaal Republic under the guiding hand of Germany. It will be lucky if Europe succeeds in avoiding war as a result of the present crisis. The next time a Servian crisis arises . . ., I feel sure that Austria-Hungary will refuse to admit of any Russian interference in the dispute and that she will proceed to settle her differences with her little neighbor by herself 'coûte que coûte.'"[17]

[17]Sir F. Cartwright to Sir A. Nicolson, January 31, 1913, G. P. Gooch and Harold Temperley, ed., *British Documents on the Origins of the War 1898–1914*, IX, part II (London, 1934), p. 467.

Had Belgrade not been bidding for a Greater Serbia, there could have been a way out even after the Austrian ultimatum. Pašić, in the case, could have upset all of Austria's plans by accepting the ultimatum *in toto*. "Such an acceptance would have made it impossible for the Austrians, in the eyes of world opinion, to start a war, and the few Austrian officials dispatched to Serbia to investigate the assassination would have provided a perfect spectacle of helplessness. The claim that such a mission could not be reconciled with the Serbian constitution cannot be taken very seriously. Worse things had happened in Serbia that were not in accord with the constitution."[18]

No, the reason some Serbians were willing to play the game the way the Austrians wished them to was that they thought the prize justified the stakes, and that with Russia's aid chances were good that the prize might be won. Nor did they play the game at all badly. Their reply to the ultimatum was a triumph—but it was a triumph in public relations rather than in settling the crisis. Which was what Belgrade had in mind. The pursuit of Serbia's aims was worth a war with Austria. And if that war should activate Europe's alliances, and bring about an Austro-German-Serbian-Russian-French war, so be it. No fears of international complications, after all, had been capable of forestalling two earlier Balkan Wars. Turkey was dying and now Austria was. 1914–1918 was the longest but by no means the only war of the Turkish succession. It was the Third Balkan War.

Overlooking Belgrade stands the great Yugoslav World War I memorial, the tomb of the unknown soldier. A vast flight of steps leads up to a sort of temple where eight female figures in black marble represent the nations of Yugoslavia: Serbia, Croatia, Dalmatia, Bosnia, and the rest. On the floor, there is a single inscription, which reads:

1912–1918

Seen that way, Serbia was wholly right in the decision of July 25, and the question of "war guilt" becomes unreal and irrelevant. Of course, so was everybody, right, and one wishes that Versailles had never introduced the concept of guilt. Serbia was right in wanting to expand, Austria in wanting to survive. Germany was right in fearing isolation, Great Britain in fearing German power. Everyone was

[18] Golo Mann, *Deutsche Geschichte des 19. und 20. Jahrhunderts* (Frankfurt, 1969), p. 580.

right. And everyone was wrong, for no one foresaw what war would mean, either in terms of costs or of consequences. All were sinners, all were sinned against.

But then, discussions of causes, like so many other things in history, are constructions after the event. How many people, in 1914, were really that aware of all the origins of the conflict, immediate and long-range, that we abstract in leisure from the documents later? How many had thought through every move of the diplomatic game, from Princip's opening to checkmate? Not even Berchtold or Pašić. What most of them did feel—and act on—was that here was another crisis, one that contained great risks obviously, but that might reasonably be expected to end as non-cataclysmically as the diplomatic crises of the past decades had. That it did not, that this time, the rhetoric of war would be followed by the reality, none of them foresaw, let alone planned. Only prophets after the event would be able to see the inevitability of arriving, step by step, stage by stage, by a series of moves and countermoves that all seemed logical, reasonable, and containable at the time, at a road which had no turns left. And perhaps, all one can truly say in the end is that World War I was a modern diplomatic crisis gone wrong, the one gamble, or rather series of gambles, that did not work out, the one deterrent that did not deter. It happens.

II WITNESSES

3 FROM *Gavrilo Princip*

Some, of course, had contributed more than others to making it happen. In October 1914, the Austrians put on trial the Sarajevo assassins and their helpers. In the court session of October 12, Gavrilo Princip (b. 1894) recalled what had taken place three and a half months earlier.

The Defendant: . . . The car approached me and I heard the detonation of the bomb. I knew that a member of our group must have thrown it, but I did not know which one. The crowd began to move, and I moved with it for a bit. The cars had stopped. I thought that all was over, and I saw how Čabrinović[1] was being led away. The thought flashed through my mind to kill him so the matter would be closed. But as I saw the cars start on their way again, I abandoned the idea. At that moment, I could not make out the archduke. I did see a lady seated next to him, but they went by very fast and her presence made no particular impression on me. I went toward the Lateiner Bridge and heard people say that the attempt had failed. Now I asked myself where I should take up my post. I had read the itinerary in the *Bosanska Posta* and in the *Tagblatt*.

I stopped. A certain Pušara came up to me and said, "have you seen this foolishness?" I made no response. He drew me aside. I thought

SOURCE. Albert Mousset, Ed., *Un drame historique, L'attentat de Sarajevo, Documents inédits et texte intégral des sténogrammes du procès* (Paris: Éditions Payot, 1930), pp. 129–130. Reprinted by permission of the publisher. The translation of this selection, as well as of all subsequent passages from the French and German, unless otherwise noted, was made by Joachim Remak for this volume.

[1] Nedjelko Čabrinović, a year younger than Princip, who had thrown the bomb at Franz Ferdinand's car, and missed.

that he might be a police spy, and felt that he wished to make me talk. One of his parents is a spy and I figured that he was one too.[2] I don't know if he was still close to me when the car passed by again. I drew my gun and fired twice at [Franz] Ferdinand, at a distance of four or five feet.

Presiding Judge: The second time, did you see the lady?

Def.: No. What I saw was that there was someone else in the car still, and I wanted to kill Potiorek.[3]

Pr. Judge: Did you know that your shots had gone home?

Def.: No. I did not even know how many bullets I had fired. I raised my arm to commit suicide, but policemen and officers grabbed me and beat me, in order to pay me back for what I had done. They led me away all covered with blood to the police station, where I was kicked and beaten again.[4]

4 FROM *Dragutin Dimitrijević, Called Apis*

Not everyone connected with the assassination came from the Austrian side of the border. Most prominent among those on the Serbian side was Colonel Dragutin Dimitrijević, called Apis, the bee. Dimitrijević (b. 1887) was chief of Serbian army intelligence, and, in his spare time, one of the leading members of a secret society named Union or Death, a society better known, to the extent that it was known, as the Black Hand. It was the Black Hand that was behind many of the activities in Bosnia—from the collection of information to the distribution of propaganda and of arms—which had so exasperated the Austrians even before Sarajevo.

In 1917, for reasons that are still not wholly clear, Apis' own government put him on trial for an alleged attempt on the life of the Serbian Crown Prince, Alexander. During the trial, Apis submitted the following document to the court. Many of its details are subject to debate. Thus the document may exaggerate the Sarajevo role

SOURCE. Stoyan Gabrilović, "New Evidence on the Sarajevo Assassination," *The Journal of Modern History*, Vol. 27, No. 4 (December 1955), pp. 410–411. Reprinted by permission of The University of Chicago Press.

[2] Princip is successfully protecting a friend here. Actually, Mihajlo Pušara was a participant in the conspiracy.

[3] The Austrian governor of Bosnia-Herzegovina.

[4] On October 29, Princip, along with the other major defendants, was found guilty. Since Austrian law precluded the death penalty for anyone under twenty, and Princip was four weeks short of that birthday (most of the others were even younger) he was sentenced to prison, where he died, in 1917, of tuberculosis.

of his fellow defendant Malobabić, in order to gain the latter the sympathy of the court. There also remains some question about the extent of Russia's advance knowledge, as well as promises, concerning Sarajevo. But the gist of the document, and particularly of Apis' role in the affair, seems to be correct.

TO THE MILITARY TRIBUNAL FOR OFFICERS

From the writ of accusation in the matter of the attempt on the life of His Royal Highness the crown prince, I have seen that the guilt for that attempt is laid upon Rade Malobabić[1] and Muhamed Mehmedbašić[2] and that I myself am accused of complicity in that deed. My participation in this deed is based primarily on my great personal interest in both accused and my constant intercessions in their behalf.

Being forced thus to justify before the tribunal by the real reasons this interest on my part, I shall have to bring to light a circumstance which binds me to the two accused and on account of which I have shown them so much consideration. In fact, I must explain why I am in conscience bound to stand by these two persons.

The situation is as follows:

Rade Malobabić is the man whom I engaged in my capacity as chief of the intelligence division of the general staff to organize my intelligence network in Austria-Hungary and who undertook to do this for me. This I did in agreement with the Russian military attaché, Mr. Artamanov, who also had personal interviews with Rade in my presence. Once Rade had started with the execution of this assignment, and feeling that Austria was making preparations for war against us, I thought that with the disappearance of the Austrian Heir Apparent Ferdinand, the party and the climate of opinion he headed would lose its impetus and that in that way the danger of war would be removed from Serbia or at any rate would be postponed. Accordingly, I engaged Malobabić to organize an attempt on Ferdinand's life on the occasion of his announced visit to Sarajevo. I decided this definitely only after Artamanov gave me assurances that Russia would not leave us without protection if Austria attacked us. To Mr. Artamanov on this occasion I did not impart any information on

[1] A fellow member of the Black Hand, and one of Apis' top agents in Austria-Hungary.

[2] One of the seven assassins at Sarajevo.

my plans regarding the assassination. To make my demand for his opinion as to the attitude of Russia well founded, I pretended that our intelligence activities might be detected, so that this also might be made to serve as an excuse for Austria to attack us. Malobabić completed the mission I assigned to him. He organized and carried out the assassination. His principal aides were in my service. They had a small honorarium which I was sending them through Malobabić. Some of their signed receipts are in Russian hands, since I was receiving the money I needed for this work from Artamanov. The general staff at that time did not have funds for these expanded operations.

Muhamed Mehmedbašić is the only Muslim[3] Serb who was a participant in this assassination and who succeeded in escaping first to Montenegro and then, during the war, he came to me in Užice. In addition to this, he went from Corfu to Athens with my co-operation in connection with the matter which is known on the tribunal from the preliminary investigations.

Having been bound to these two men by such great moral obligations, I did everything I could for them without thinking much of rules and regulations.

I have also especially sheltered Rade Malobabić because the chief of the police section of the supreme command headquarters, Mr. Tucaković, even before the war, at a time when he was *načelnik*[4] of the district of Podrinje, had endeavored to represent Rade as a suspect character because Rade had refused to disclose to him what he was doing with the general staff, and especially when Rade, contrary to his wishes, with the assistance of army officers stationed along the frontier, smuggled into Bosnia the bombs, the pistols, and the ammunition needed for the assassination. Also, because Mr. Malobabić, on one occasion, had already been the victim of this attitude on the part of the police, having gone through terrible ordeals, during a period of one year or more, in the police prisons in Niš. In regard to this, there were also written records of the acts of officials.

Since all this contains a considerable number of elements which are embarassing to the interests of the state and since I am forced to reveal this in my own defense as well as in the defense of the principal accused in the matter of the attempt upon the life of His Royal

[3] All the others were Serb-Orthodox.

[4] Head of the administration.

Highness the crown prince, I consider, as a Serb, that it is my duty to communicate this to the tribunal in advance.

To desist from this intention is not possible for me because I believe that the preliminary investigation, having commenced with me, has been guided precisely by these unexplained points pertaining to my associations with Mr. Malobabić in order to construe the set of circumstances which has brought him and Mr. Muhamed Mehmedbašić to the accused chair, and I could not even lie peacefully in my grave if I were to think that for no matter what reason I have permitted a Serbian military tribunal for officers to complete and put the finishing touches to the verdict rendered by the Austrian tribunal in Sarajevo and that I have let this occasion be used by a Serbian court of justice to convict the *only* Serb of Muslim faith who was a participant in the protest of the Serbian people and youth in Bosnia against the Austro-Hungarian tyranny perpetrated upon the Serbian race.

28 March 1917 — *Accused,*
In Salonika — DRAG. T. DIMITRIJEVIĆ
Colonel, General Staff

5 FROM *Johannes Urzidil*

Not all these details of course, were known in 1914. Yet even so, it seemed apparent to many that the one irreconcilable conflict in Europe was that between Austria and Serbia. And when that conflict turned into war, there were few public regrets. Johannes Urzidil (b. 1896) a German writer from Prague, was vacationing in the spa of Karlsbad when the Austro-Serbian crisis came to a head. His recollections remind us how euphoric the mood of Europe could be in 1914, and with what innocence that mood was exchanged for another.

. . . On the morning of June 22, when I took my package to the main post office in Karlsbad, the famous resort town was still its usual lively self. Americans, Frenchmen, Britishers, Russians (who had a special love for Karlsbad) could be seen and heard everywhere. It was the sort of public which had made this small town into a

SOURCE. Johannes Urzidil, "Der Kriegsauchbruch," *Der Monat*, Vol. 16, No. 190 (August 1964), pp. 40–41. Reprinted by permission of the publisher.

brilliant international center, into an intellectual and political crossroads of the world even in Goethe's day. The luxurious shop windows were full of expensive goods. People were promenading under the colonnades that led to the fountains, or on the elegant "Old Meadow," or they were sitting at the tables of Pupp's Café at the foot of the Goethe monument. (Naive visitor's question: "Who's that?" Answer: "Who do you think it is? Old man Pupp of course.") Or else one would walk down the valley path which Goethe, too, had often taken, to the Mail Coach Inn, which looked hardly any different from the way it did in the drawing he made of it in 1807.

Toward the evening of the 23rd, there was a mild feeling of tension, as Berchtold's ultimatum to Serbia became known. There were stories that some Russians had begun to pack their bags. But most of the visitors came from the area of the Dual Monarchy and from Central Europe, and were convinced that Serbia would bow to Austrian pressure. After all, Austria and Germany were Giants both, marching side by side, allies, friends, helpers. How could a little country half the size of Cuba defy them? Thus people went on enjoying themselves.

Among the entertainments was a benefit concert given in the garden of the Great Hall on the afternoon of July 28, a Tuesday. I went, for admission was cheap, and included refreshments. A Count Kolowrat, of terribly ancient Bohemian nobility, was in charge of the benefit, and among the honored guests was none less than the archduchess Elizabeth, granddaughter of the emperor, and daughter of that tragic figure, crown prince Rudolf. A military band played tunes by Lehár, Waldteufel, Zierer, and Josef Strauss (Josef, let me emphasize that; I can still hear the caressing sounds of the Waltz of the Village Swallows). . . . There even was a raffle, in which a terribly pretty French girl who, parents included, ornamented the table next to mine, won the grand prize. It was a necklace of genuine pearls, which the donor, Count Kolowrat, presented to her. She was jubilant—"*le grand prix, le grand prix*," all in tones of pure silver. I thought her as beautiful as any heroine in a novel by Francis Jammes, and much more important, at that moment, than any ultimatum or ambassadors' conference. She was introduced to the archduchess, who held out an infinitely long, white gloved hand to her.

In short, it all was suffused by Austrian magic still, a melody of charm, which accompanied me throughout the evening. The hours passed as quickly as they will when one is dreaming about all the enticing details surrounding a lovely and unattainable girl now wearing a count's pearls.

Thus night came, and I aimlessly wandered through the now quiet town. On the "Old Meadow," I suddenly was stopped by a crowd of people which, straight and motionless, surrounded a tobacco and newspaper kiosk. My curiosity impelled me to force a way through and there, on the door, was a telegram.

"War Declared."

Nobody spoke. Then I suddenly heard the words

"Thank God."

The man who spoke them was an Austrian first lieutenant. . . .

6 FROM *Sergei Sazonov*

There were less jubilant voices, too. Among the diplomats, in particular, there were some who had clearer perception of what the coming years would bring. Sergei Sazonov (1861–1927), Russia's foreign minister, has described the last call that the German ambassador, Count Friedrich von Pourtalès, paid him on August 1, 1914.

. . . Count Pourtalès came to see me at seven o'clock in the evening, and after the very first few words asked me whether the Russian Government was ready to give a favorable answer to the ultimatum presented the day before. I answered in the negative, observing that although general mobilization could not be cancelled, Russia was nevertheless disposed, as before, to continue negotiations with a view to a peaceful settlement.

Count Pourtalès was much agitated. He repeated his question, dwelling upon the serious consequences which our refusal to comply with the German request would involve. I gave the same answer. Pulling out of his pocket a folded sheet of paper, the Ambassador repeated his question for the third time in a voice that trembled. I said that I could give no other answer. Deeply moved, the Ambassador said to me, speaking with difficulty:

"In that case my Government charges me to give you the following note."

SOURCE. Serge Sazonov, *The Fateful Years, 1909–1916, The Reminiscences of Serge Sazonov*, M. A. Duddington, trans. (London: Jonathan Cape Ltd., 1928), pp. 212–213. Reprinted by permission of the publisher.

And with a shaking hand Pourtalès handed me the Declaration of War. It contained two versions which, through an oversight of the German Embassy, were included in the same text. I did not notice this at the time, for the meaning of the note was perfectly obvious and I did not have time at the moment to go over it word for word.

After handing the note to me, the Ambassador, who had found it a great strain to carry out his orders, lost all self-control and leaning against the window burst into tears. With a gesture of despair he repeated: "Who could have thought that I should be leaving St. Petersburg under such circumstances!"

In spite of my own emotion, which I managed to overcome, I felt sincerely sorry for him. We embraced each other and with tottering steps he walked out of the room. . . .

7 FROM *Alphonse Grasset*

But the overwhelming mood in Europe was one of relief, even of jubilation. "Thank God. . . ." The way Europe went to war in 1914 tells us much about why it went to war, it reveals reasons that often elude us in the standard diplomatic or political accounts of the war's origins. Few tears; instead crowds in Vienna, crowds in St. Petersburg, crowds in Berlin, crowds in Belgrade, wildly enthusiastic all. (We have a photograph of the Munich crowd in which we can recognize an ecstatic young Hitler. He had company.)

The fact was that many people were bored with peace; there had been too much of it. People were tired of living in an atmosphere of perpetual diplomatic crisis; let arms decide the issues, once and for all, even if few people might be able to tell just what the issues were. People—not all, but surely most of them—had a profound sense of being in the right; they felt that their side, and their side only, had truth and justice written on its banners. And people were convinced that it was their banners that would prevail. "This Christmas in Paris," was the cry in Berlin, "this Christmas in Berlin" that in Paris. Emotions such as these were as much cause of the war as my single crisis or any specific point of diplomatic contention. And they were suffused with genuine love of country, surely not the worst of emotions, which now came pouring out.

This was true even of the power least responsible for the war—France. Commandant

SOURCE. Commandant A. Grasset, *Vingt Jours de Guerre aux Temps Héroiques* (Paris: Berger-Levrault, 1918), pp. 36–39. Reprinted by permission of the publisher.

Alphonse Grasset (1873–), French army major, military historian, and battalion commander, has given us this account of what he felt and saw as he and his men left for the front that summer.

August 8. . . . In a few words, the commanding officer tells the battalion what needs to be said. His conclusion, "Love each other," echoes from the three walls of the old military academy, and for a moment reminds every one of us of the solemnity of this supreme leave-taking.

Where shall we be tomorrow? How many of us will still be alive a month from now? How many, after victory, will have the joy of returning to this courtyard and to march, heads high, eyes straight, to the sound of cheers and to the stirring rythmn of a triumphal march?

Outside, the crowd is packed tight before the fence; parents and friends have come. The crowd opens up to let us through. No shouts, no demonstrations; one senses a deep emotion in the air. Discreetly, a few shadows detach themselves from the dark mass and follow us.

The streets are far from empty. Paris is not asleep. We pass the rue Mignon, and I look. All is calm as usual. I am happy to see that the shutters of my apartment are tightly closed. My family is gone. They are safe; far from any surprise or danger or want. I feel at ease. It seems to me that the sacrifice of my very being, which I owe, costs me nothing, and I understand now why some countries, born of war and for war, will not let their officers marry.

There is a lively crowd at the Vaugirard station. . . . Gently and without any signal, the train begins to move at 6 A.M. At that moment, spontaneously, like a smoldering fire that suddenly erupts into roaring flames, an immense clamor arises—the *Marseilleise* bursts from a thousand throats. The men all are standing at the train's windows, waving their caps. From tracks and platforms and from neighboring trains the crowd responds.

It is an impressive moment. The heart of a great nation, liberated finally, is beating, beating, as it did in days past. If Kaiser Wilhelm could have witnessed our departure, no doubt he would have felt uneasy about the consequences of his adventure.

I shall not try to describe our journey to Verdun; sunshine cannot be reproduced on canvas.

The wildest enthusiasm reigns. The songs of the nation, the

Marseilleise, Chant du Départ, Hymne des Girondins follow each other without interruption, to the exclusion of anything else.

As if by magic, our train has been decked with flowers and flags. No one knows who has put them there; one might believe that they had fallen from heaven.

There are crowds gathered at every station, behind every barrier, and at every house that borders the tracks. Everywhere cries of "*Vive la France! Vive l'armée!*"—brisk and vibrant. The women were throwing kisses, and showering flowers on our convoy. The young men were shouting, "*Au revoir! à bientôt!*" At one grade crossing, a young woman held her baby toward us, shouting, "He'll be going there too, like you. He'll do his duty."

During forty years of peace, we had been taught, in France, to consider such shows of emotion vulgar and ridiculous. But their time had come again, and to all of us who were there, they gave a feeling both grand and sublime; our eyes filled with tears. . . .

PART TWO
The War

They are not soldiers, they are men. They are not adventurers, or warriors, or made for human slaughter, neither butchers nor cattle. They are laborers and craftsmen whom one recognizes in their uniforms. They are civilians uprooted, and they are ready. They await the signal for death or murder; but you may see, looking at their faces between the vertical gleams of their bayonets, that they are simply men.

Each one knows that he is going to take his head, his chest, his stomach, his whole body, and all naked, up to the rifles pointed forward, to the shells, to the bombs piled and ready, and above all to the methodical and almost infallible machine-guns—to everything that is waiting for him over there and is now so frightfully silent—before he reaches the other soldiers that he must kill. They are not careless of their lives, like outlaws, nor blinded by passion, like savages. In spite of the propaganda with which they have been belabored, they are not incensed. They are above instinctive excesses. They are not drunk, either physically or morally. It is in full consciousness, as in full health and full strength, that they are massed there to hurl themselves once more into that sort of madman's part imposed on all men by the madness of the human race. One sees the dream and the fear and the farewell that there is in their silence, their stillness, in the mask of tranquillity which unnaturally grips their faces. They are not the kind of hero one thinks of, but their sacrifice has greater worth than those who have not seen them will ever be able to understand.

HENRI BARBUSSE, *Le Feu*

III HISTORIANS

To give a detailed description of the entire military conduct of the war on all its fronts would clearly go beyond the limits of this volume. But to describe it in its major outlines, to place it in perspective, and to give some indication of the technical and political changes that it brought does not. The selection that follows is such an attempt, undertaken by a man who was master at seeing things whole as well as in detail.

8 FROM *Bernadotte E. Schmitt. The First World War, 1914–1918*

Bernadotte Schmitt (1886–1969), Rhodes scholar, Pulitzer prize winner, professor at the University of Chicago from 1914 to 1946, and president of the American Historial Association in 1960, is best known for his The Coming of the War, 1914. *In that book, he refused—in contrast to Sidney B. Fay and the revisionists—to absolve the Central Powers from the major part of the responsibility for the war. Schmitt also was an expert on the Balkan background of the conflict, and on the war itself. The paper from which a major selection is printed here was delivered on the occasion of the fortieth anniversary of the armistice.*

. . . So we come to the war itself. The expectation was widespread that the struggle would be brief. For one thing, it was often argued that modern war would be too expensive for governments to wage for a long time. The view derived from Norman Angell's famous book *The Great Illusion* published in 1910. Angell did not say, as is some-

SOURCE. Bernadotte E. Schmitt, "The First World War, 1914–1918," *Proceedings of the American Philosophical Society*, Vol. 103, No. 3 (June 1959), pp. 324–330. Reprinted by permission of the American Philosophical Society.

times alleged, that economics would make war impossible. What he did say was that war would be ruinous to both victor and vanquished, and it was precisely for this reason that banking interests in July 1914 lifted their voices against the oncoming catastrophe.

More positive evidence of belief in a short war is the fact that no government had made serious economic preparation for war. In no country had reserves of food, fuel, or raw materials been accumulated. The German general staff believed that, if the neutrality of Holland were respected, Germany would be able to import freely through the Dutch ports. It was not until after the war had begun that the general staff addressed itself to the problem of organizing Germany's resources for war. Britain never had on hand food supplies for more than a few months, yet relied on the ability of the navy to control the seas and allow supplies to come in. In no belligerent country did the rationing of food begin until long after the opening of hostilities.

On the military side, it was the same story. The German general staff expected to defeat France in six or seven weeks—and they jolly well nearly succeeded!—and then turn on Russia, which was expected to collapse in a few months. This pre-war optimism of the Germans was matched on the Allied side after the war started, when there was much talk of the Russian "steam roller" getting to Berlin by Christmas. Lord Kitchener, the famous British soldier who was appointed secretary for war on the outbreak of hostilities, was not taken too seriously when he said that the war would last at least three years. Most interesting of all, no general staff had the least conception of the consumption of ammunition. By September, only a few weeks after the fighting had begun, the generals on both sides were complaining of the shortage of shells, although it had been assumed that there were supplies for months of campaigning. Apparently no government had planned in advance to make the enormous quantities of ammunition consumed by the war.

By the end of 1914, instead of the Germans getting to Paris or the Russians to Berlin, the war had reached a stalemate in Belgium and France. The rival offensives of the French and German armies had both failed, and trench warfare had set in. This trench warfare lasted from November 1914 to March 1918. For more than three years millions of men on both sides lived in trenches fortified with concrete and defended by machine guns and mortars in the front line and by heavy artillery at the rear. The British and French generals, and to a considerable extent the German generals as well, managed to convince themselves that, if only enough shells were fired at the enemy trenches, these footholds could be demolished and then the infantry could go forward to seize the rubble that was left. The mirage of "break-through" fascinated equally Joffre and Haig and Falkenhayn, the principal French, British, and German commanders during the first two years of the war, and, in spite of repeated failures and enormous losses, they never admitted to themselves that the thing could not be done. In several instances cavalry was massed behind the lines to dash through into the open country. The inability of the professional soldiers to find a way out of this deadlock reflects rather sadly on their imagination. It is no wonder that a famous Frenchman, Georges Clemenceau, is reported to have said, after he became premier in 1917, that war was much too serious a business to be entrusted to generals.

If our Civil War was the first conflict in which railroads were used on a large scale, the First World War witnessed the *début* of the internal combustion engine. In land warfare, the gasoline engine was applied in three ways. First, from the beginning of operations motor trucks were used to transport troops, guns, ammunition, and supplies beyond the railheads, and sometimes, as at Verdun, this was the only means of transport to the immediate fighting zone.

Second, the airplane was used for the first time in war. At the beginning, it was used only for reconnaissance, for it was an untried weapon and there were only about five hundred planes in all the armies put together. Gradually it began to be used for locating trenches and "spotting" artillery fire. Then troops were bombed from low-flying planes, and ultimately high-flying planes were employed for general bombing. Not only this, but planes fought each other for the control of the air, which slowly but surely passed to the Allies, who were able to make more planes, thousands of them, than the Germans. This superiority did not, however, enable the Allies to overcome the advantage possessed by the Germans, who were, on the whole, content to remain on the defensive and let the Allies exhaust themselves in fruitless assaults against the trenches. These assaults did yield the Allies a few square miles of territory, but in March 1918, the line had changed little from November 1914, and the German armies were still firmly entrenched in Belgium and France.

The deadlock on the western front was in the end broken by the mechanical contraption which we call the tank. The conception of a self-propelling vehicle which could cross trenches and also shoot came from the brain of a subordinate British officer serving in France; this was the third application of the gasoline engine to the revolutionizing of warfare. But it was long resisted by the generals and it was carried through to execution largely by civilian initiative. Even after they had been converted to the idea and had begun to use the tanks in France, the generals refused to employ the tactics prescribed by the inventor, and it was not until November 1917 that the tank came into its own at the battle of Cambrai. Even then, the top German commander, the famous Ludendorff, was not impressed and failed to build German tanks in adequate quantities or to devise adequate defenses against it. Open warfare returned with the great German attack in the West in March 1918, and, thanks to superior numbers at the outset and to the use of liquid fire, they were able to break through. But when the Allies, now reinforced by the American armies, rallied, they possessed in the tank the weapon which enabled them to defeat the Germans. The Germans proved unable to improvise sufficient resistance, and being unable to defend their positions, they lost the war.

The war on the Eastern front was quite different from that in the West—"the unknown war," Sir Winston Churchill has called it. The territory fought over was vastly larger than the compact area of the West, and trench warfare never developed. The Russian army was large but after the first few weeks, short of munitions. The Austro-Hungarian army was a hodge-podge of rival nationalities, some of which were not loyal and deserted to the enemy in large numbers. Generally speaking, the Russians were able to defeat the Austrians, but were themselves beaten by the Germans. By the end of 1915 the Russians had been defeated and driven out of Poland and, although they made a brief comeback in 1916, they had suffered so greatly that by 1917 they were ripe for revolution.

Yet we must not underestimate the part played by the Russian army in the war. In the opening campaign, the Russians chivalrously invaded East Prussia, in order to help their French allies, and, although they were badly defeated, they so scared the German general staff that it detached two corps from the German armies in the West and sent them eastwards. Had these troops been available for the battle of the Marne, which stopped the German army before Paris, the result might have been different. Later, even after the Russians had been defeated, the German general staff never dared denude the Russian front and throw all its forces into the battle in France. I have often wondered what would have happened if in 1914 Germany had stood on the defensive in the West and launched its big offensive against Russia. Probably the German army could have stopped the

French offensive, and certainly, if Belgium had been left alone, Britain would not have entered the war at the start.

The most spectacular incident of the war was the campaign at the Dardanelles. This arose out of a Russian request to have the Turkish pressure in the Caucasus relieved, which came at the moment when the Allied leaders were seeking a way out of the trench warfare in the West. Strategically, the concept was sound, for success would not only have put Turkey out of the war but would have opened up a route to Russia for easier than the difficult voyage to Archangel. It would take too long to list the numerous mistakes by which the expedition was bungled from the start. In spite of these errors, success was narrowly missed. After the great naval attack of March 18, 1915, the Turkish ammunition was exhausted and plans were made to evacuate the peninsula and Constantinople when the attack was renewed the next day; but the Allied admiral had been scared by his losses and failed to go on. During the land fighting, the British almost captured the critical heights which dominated Gallipoli; but bad generalship and bad luck were too much for them. It is generally agreed that if the Allies had been able to open the Straits and supply Russia with what it needed, the Russian revolution might not have happened.

The Russian revolution of March 1917 had a double aspect. On the one hand, it was a revolt against the corruption and inefficiency of the tsarist regime, a revolt brewing for half a century and already once attempted, in 1905; on the other hand, it was a protest against continuing the war. As a movement to achieve liberty and reform, it was hailed by the Allies—"heartening news" Woodrow Wilson called it—who had always been somewhat uncomfortable about the Russian autocracy and hoped that upheaval would find echoes among the discontented peoples of the Central Powers, as indeed it did. The new order forced the Austrian government to summon the Austrian parliament, which had been in eclipse since 1914, and in Prussia loud demands began to be heard for reform of the antiquated three-class franchise. The new Russia was, to quote Wilson again, "a fit partner for a League of Honor."

The revolution as a protest against continuing the war was not understood in the West. The British and French were being hard pressed on the Western front and they refused to face the possibility of Russia's withdrawal from the war; they even believed that the revolution would strengthen Russian enthusiasm for the war. The demands of the Russian radicals for peace on the basis of no annexations and no indemnities were deeply resented, and when the Provisional Government set up in March, which was keenly aware of the groundswell calling for peace, asked for a reconsideration of war aims, no reply was returned. Under pressure from the Allies, the provisional government staged an offensive in the summer of 1917, which, though momentarily successful, was soon beaten back, and the failure not only completed the demoralization of the Russian army but also deprived the government of reliable troops with which to resist the Bolshevist attack of November 7. Whether greater understanding by the Allied governments of the Russian situation would have prevented the Bolshevist triumph, no one can say, but their actual policy played directly into the hands of the Communists. On the other hand, it is only fair to remember that if the Allies had agreed to discuss peace on the Russian terms, the Germans might have felt it safe to shift troops from the Eastern to the Western front, whereas actually they did not begin to shift troops until much later, until they had opened negotiations with the Bolshevist government.

The German general staff quickly realized that the first revolution had profoundly affected the Russian army; so it refrained from attacks and sent its own agitators, including Lenin himself, to stir up agitation among the troops. Undoubtedly the German maneuvers contributed considerably to the breakdown of the Russian army, and Germany profited at first from this. Not only was it safe to begin transferring troops to the West, but, at the end of 1917, Germany was able to open negotiations with the Bolshevist government which resulted in the Peace of Brest-Litovsk. By this treaty Russia was forced to surrender vast areas of its territory to the Central Powers and to accept harsh economic terms. The triumph of Germany seemed complete. Yet, in the end, the Germans were hoist with their own petard, for, after the establishment of diplomatic relations between Germany and the Communist government, the Russians were able to launch their Communist propaganda in Germany and this helped undermine the German will to resist in the autumn of 1918. So the Allies had no monopoly on not knowing how to deal properly with the situation created by the Russian revolution.

What were the war aims of the Allies which the Russians wished to discuss? Americans will immediately think of the secret treaties of 1915–1917, by which the Allies planned to cut back the frontiers of Germany and distributed the overseas possessions of Germany among themselves, promised parts of Austria-Hungary to Italy and Romania, awarded Constantinople to Russia and partitioned most of the Ottoman Empire. These agreements, secretly negotiated and carefully not published, were certainly not in harmony with the professions of disinterestedness and respect for the principle of self-determination which the Allies publicly proclaimed. But, in fact, they were in large measure the consequences of military situations. The promise of Constantinople to Russia was made when the Allies were trying to force the Dardanelles; if they had succeeded and captured the city, they would have aroused deep suspicion in Russia had they tried to hold it for themselves. Was it unreasonable to partition the Ottoman Empire? The Allies had offered to guarantee its integrity in return for Turkish neutrality; but Turkey had joined the enemy and vastly extended the scope of the war. The promises made to Italy and Romania were exaggerated and unjustified, but here again it seemed that the tide of battle might be turned if these new armies entered the conflict. To some extent the Allies were in the position of parents who had to ransom kidnapped children—they did not haggle too much over what they had to pay. The secret treaties contained many unjustified provisions, provisions which, when the time came to put them into effect, proved impracticable. Actually, the treaties were of less consequence than is often alleged, and since they were published by the Bolshevist government of Russia at the end of 1917, they had to face the test of public opinion.

If the Allies in 1917 lost one ally, Russia, they gained another, the United States. . . . The American contribution to the military winning of the war was very great. In France the tired British and French armies almost broke under the heavy German attacks in March 1918; it was the fresh, huge American army that provided the superiority necessary for victory. No doubt our raw troops made many mistakes which the seasoned British and French had learned to avoid, but once our troops went into action on a grand scale, the Germans, although they continued to fight well, knew that the war was lost. At sea we introduced new methods which proved successful in beating the submarine. While it would be untrue to claim that we won the war, clearly the war could not have been won without us.

American policy contributed enormously to the ending of the war in 1918. From the moment that the United States entered the war, the discontented nationalities of Austria-Hungary had looked to Wilson as the prophet of self-determination, and they were disappointed when in the Ninth of the Fourteen Points, he talked only of autonomy within the Habsburg state. At that moment, it seemed possible that the Emperor Charles might be willing to negotiate for a separate peace, so Wilson had to be cautious. But the negotiations came to naught, and presently the United States recognized publicly the claims for independence and unity of the Czechoslovaks, Jugoslavs, and Poles, the three most important minorities of Austria-Hungary. This was the beginning of the end. At the beginning of September, the Austro-Hungarian government, now *in extremis*, appealed to Wilson for the opening of peace negotiations on the basis of the Ninth Point, only to be told that the Ninth Point had been overtaken by events. In other words, the United States no longer stood for autonomy or federalization within Austria-Hungary but sanctioned its destruction. This was the signal for which the nationalities had been waiting, and when the Austrian army was defeated by the Italians at Vittorio Veneto, first the Czechs and then the Jugoslavs, and finally even the Magyars declared their independence. When the armistice with Italy was signed on November 3, the Austro-Hungarian state had ceased to exist. The Czechs honored their liberator by naming the principal railway station in Praha for Wilson.

On October 4, after the Allied armies had broken the Hindenburg Line in France, the German government appealed to Wilson for an armistice, this to be the preliminary to a peace based on the Fourteen Points. Just previous to this the Kaiser, by a stroke of the pen, had taken the revolutionary step of making the imperial chancellor responsible to the Reichstag. The proposal for an armistice emanated from the general staff, not from the civil government, which realized that peace on the basis of the Fourteen Points would signify defeat for Germany, and the new chancellor, Prince Max of Baden, opposed the move. Ludendorff, however, was adamant, and the appeal was made. But Ludendorff was not sincere. He was playing for time, in hope of reconstituting the German armies and fighting on. Wilson sensed this and acted accordingly. In a series of notes, about which he did not consult the Allies, he demanded that the German armies evacuate all Allied territory and stop the submarine warfare; he also challenged the authority of the German government and declared that the Allies could negotiate only with a democratic regime. Finally he stated that, if he had to negotiate with the military rulers and the monarchical autocrats of Germany, he must insist not on negotiations but on surrender. Pushed from one position to another and realizing the hopelessness of a *levée en masse* as urged by Ludendorff, the German government accepted all of Wilson's conditions. This masterly diplomatic achievement, done publicly, was accomplished in the face of considerable criticism at home and in the Allied countries, where it was feared that Wilson would let the Germans off too easily.

All things considered, this must be reckoned Wilson's most brilliant performance.

American diplomacy was equally effective in dealing with the Allies. When Wilson communicated to them his correspondence with the German government, they were reluctant to accept the Fourteen Points, but Wilson's representative in Paris, Colonel House, threatened that, in case of refusal, the United States might negotiate a separate peace with Germany. Whether House was authorized to say this or did it on his own responsibility is not clear; but the effect was magical: the Allies accepted the Fourteen Points, with two reservations. The American commander, General Pershing, was opposed to an armistice, but the British and French commanders favored it, and Marshal Foch, the commander-in-chief, asserted that if the Germans accepted his conditions, they would be rendered powerless. Wilson, for the only time, did not back up Pershing and followed Foch. The Germans did accept the Allied terms, and the war came to an end on November 11, 1918.

Or rather it came almost to an end. During 1918 Allied troops had landed on Russian soil at Archangel, in the Caucasus and in Siberia. The alleged object of these expeditions was to protect Allied interests against Germany, but the Bolshevist government regarded them as directed against itself and it broke off relations with the Allies. In October, however, as the war was nearing its end, the Bolshevist government addressed itself to Wilson and proposed negotiations. No answer was sent to this communication. But the armistice did require Germany to denounce the Treaty of Brest-Litovsk and to withdraw its troops from Russia. The Allies hoped that the Bolshevist regime would be overthrown (for civil war was already raging in Russia) and they were trying to safeguard their relations with a future "white" regime. Thus at the end of the war, the position of Russia remained uncertain.

The war of 1914–1918 was the bloodiest and most costly yet fought in modern times. Exact figures of the casualties are not obtainable and, on so vast a scale, do not matter. It is safe to say that about ten million were killed, something like twenty million were wounded, and another six or seven million were listed as prisoners or missing. The money cost has been estimated as in excess of two hundred billion dollars. In addition, vast areas in Belgium and northern France, Poland, Russia, and the Balkans were devastated and millions of tons of shipping were lost at sea. The people of all the warring countries in Europe suffered hardships on a scale hitherto unknown. Until the greater losses and suffering of the Second World War had to be endured, it was believed that human patience had been pushed to the limit. In the minds of governments and people alike the losses and the sufferings were justified by the belief, or at least the hope, that they were the necessary preliminaries to the New and Better World that was to emerge from the war. When, later, it became doubtful whether a better world had emerged, many asked the question whether it would not have been wiser, instead of fighting the war to a finish, to have negotiated a compromise peace. That was Wilson's original idea, the explanation of his phrase "peace without victory." It was only after Germany had double-crossed him at the beginning of 1917 that he swung over to the view that Germany had to be beaten down. When the German government proposed peace negotiations at the end of 1916, Hohenzollern, Habsburg, and Romanov still sat upon their thrones and the framework of European society had not been shattered; Communism had not yet come to power in Russia. But the German terms, as made known secretly to Wilson, were not the terms of compromise. Nor were the Allied terms, as publicly stated, the terms of compromise. What Wilson might have accomplished, had he been able to play his hand, no one can say. So it came about that the war was fought to a finish. The Central Powers were overwhelmed, and, when the Allied governments assembled at Paris in January 1919, to make peace and to create the New World, they had pretty much a free hand. . . .

9 FROM *George F. Kennan* *The Price We Paid for War*

". . . the bloodiest and the most costly. . . " Starting from premises different from those of Schmitt, rejecting the idea of Germany's or any other power's principal "guilt" for 1914, George Kennan has offered some thoughts on the nature and meaning of the carnage that also go beyond the issues that sometimes tended to monopolize the attention of the war generation. Kennan (b. 1904), diplomat (director of the State Department's policy planning staff, ambassador to the U.S.S.R. and Yugoslavia) and scholar (Russia

SOURCE. George F. Kennan, "The Price We Paid for War," *The Atlantic Monthly*, Vol. 214, No. 4 (October 1964), pp. 52–54. Reprinted by permission of the publisher and the author.

Leaves the War, the Decision to Intervene, Russia and the West Under Lenin and Stalin) *wrote this article on the occasion of another anniversary, that of Sarajevo fifty years later.*

. . . Such, in the main, were the political origins of the war. They point, as one can readily see, to the conclusion that none of the four greatest continental powers involved was without blame in the complicated process of its origins. But behind these specific political circumstances, there was a deeper deficiency which lay in the spirit and the outlooks of the time and pervaded the diplomacy of all four of these powers. This was the disparity between the real implications and possibilities of major warfare as an instrument of policy in the modern age, and what people supposed these implications and possibilities to be.

The international society of that day was still dominated by romantic concepts of warfare, and these concepts embraced two great errors. First, they exaggerated the role of personal bravery and determination in a war fought with modern weapons. Under the influence of this misimpression, they pictured warfare too much as a test of the personal qualities and spirit of a nation and too little as a test of its manpower and resources and its capacity for social discipline. It was thought that if a nation's people were brave enough, spirited enough, determined enough, a nation won. People failed to realize that in a war where military realities would be governed so extensively by the machine gun and barbed wire, excessive personal valor would be only a wasteful form of foolhardiness; victory or defeat would depend primarily on the grisly mathematics of mutual destruction and, above all, on who was prepared to expend and to sacrifice the greatest quantity of men and matériel. In many of the offensives undertaken in that war, it could be, and was, calculated in advance that so and so many tens of thousands of men, one's own men as well as those of the enemy, would inevitably perish in the course of the offensive. They would perish from shells and bullets fired by men whom they could not even see. It would make no difference, or very little difference, whether they were brave as lions; they would perish anyway. War was no longer a matter just of valor and enthusiasm.

This lesson could have been learned, one would think, from the Russo-Japanese War. It does not seem to have been. As a result, governments moved lightheartedly into the horror of war in 1914, and millions of young men went singing to their death, encouraged to believe that they were embarking on a great martial adventure, as in the days of chivalry.

Second, the statesmen of the period preceding World War I had no idea of the destructiveness of modern war. They had no idea how long it would last or how many lives and resources it would consume. They deceived themselves in believing that the fruits of victory would easily overweigh the attendant sacrifices. But they grievously misestimated both elements. It did not occur to them that the losses of life—the losses, above all, of young life, of the flower of the male youth—would be so great that no conceivable fruits of victory could possibly justify them. No defeat could have carried with it disasters worse than the sacrifice of young manhood actually incurred in pursuit of victory. And no victory could have been so glorious as to justify this sacrifice. History reveals that every one of the warring powers would have been better off to have concluded peace in the early stages of the war *on the adversary's terms* rather than to accept the loss of life attendant on continuation of the war to 1918. This loss inflicted on each of the belligerents a subjective damage from which it could not recover, even superficially, for at least a generation. In a deeper sense, some may be said to have not fully recovered to the present day.

Any loss of young manhood on the scale that was incurred by the major belligerents in World War I inflicts both genetic and spiritual damage on the nation that incurs it. The age structure of the population is disbalanced. The spirit of the older people is terribly affected. They cannot stand this slaughter of their sons. A portion of themselves—of their taste for life, their capacity for hope—dies with those in whom so much of themselves was invested. Great damage is done to the youth, who are forced to grow up in an unsettled world without the steadying hand of the fathers. On the political scene, the continuity of the tradition is destroyed. The field is left to be contended for by the very old and the very young, among whom there is no intimacy. We shall never know how many of the troubles and failures of European civilization in the 1920's and 1930's, including the drift into a new world war, were attributable to these conditions.

All these are subjective damages which no victory could have made good, even if it had been as glorious as the statesmen of 1914 pictured it to themselves, and even if it had accorded fully with the objectives they had in mind when they entered the war. But actually, the war ended with results which nobody could have predicted, and which did not correspond at all with the aims for which the victor powers entered the war. . . .

In the damage it did to the structure of international life, and in the even deeper damage it inflicted on the biological and spiritual condition of the European peoples, World War I still looms on the historical horizon as *the* great determining tragedy of our century. There are many lessons to be gained from it for our own generation. But one stands out in importance. It is the lesson of the unsuitability of major war as an instrument of policy in the modern age. In that period of 1914 to 1918, thirty years before the development of the nuclear weapon, it was demonstrated that war, conducted in the grand manner and as a means of achieving major political objectives, was no longer a rational means of procedure. Defensive war might still have a rational purpose, as long as it remained exclusively and truly defensive and as long as one hoped for nothing from it but sheer survival. Limited war—war for limited objectives—might still have a rational purpose, provided the actual military effort could be held to modest dimensions and provided one could be sure of stopping in time. But all-out war, involving the total commitment of a nation's manpower and resources and aimed at the total destruction of an enemy's will to resist and the complete power to order his life and to shape his behavior, had already, in 1914, lost its rationale.

It had lost its rationale because of the terrible destructiveness of modern weapons, because of the enormous cost of cultivating and employing such weapons, because of the great complexity of modern society, because of the impossibility, the sheer technical impossibility, of one great country holding another great country in subjection for any long period of time and shaping its life in ways contrary to the will of the people. . . .

IV WITNESSES

10 FROM *Raymond Jubert*

But is there not some rhetorical exaggeration in the conclusion that war no longer remained a rational means of policy? Did World War I indeed prove that twentieth century warfare was nothing but unrelieved slaughter? Some of the participants thought otherwise. They saw repeated, in their own experiences, the attractions war has always held for some—a feeling of comradeship, a sense of purpose; an exhilarating awareness of coming truly alive in the midst of mortal danger. (Glenn Grey, in his book The Warriors, *recalls talking to a Frenchwoman ten years after World War II. She had suffered greatly in that war, and was now comfortably settled with her husband and son. Something was gone, however. "'My life is so unutterably boring nowadays!' she cried out. 'Anything is better than to have nothing at all happen day after day. You know that I do not love war or want it to return. But at least it made me feel alive, as I have not felt alive before or since.'")*

And 1914 to 1918 still witnessed, despite the randomness of destruction that is one of the by-products of the modern battle of materiel, great deeds of individual heroism. One such, and it is one among thousands, was a French counterattack near Verdun, in April 1916, part of the battle of Mort-Homme Ridge. Lieutenant Raymond Jubert, of the 51st Infantry Regiment (he was killed sixteen months later), recalled how he led his men in the assault.

We had lost the Mort-Homme Ridge, and it was essential that it be recaptured at once. We received the order to attack.

I have seldom seen less hesitation and more calm than at that moment. The adjutant gave the orders and we assembled without a word. We put our knapsacks down, and pick up a generous supply of cartridges, as well as additional rations for one day.

SOURCE. General Henri Colin, *La Côte 304 et le Mort-Homme 1916–1917*, Préface de M. le Maréchal Pétain (Payot, Paris, 1934), pp. 52–55. Reprinted by permission of the publishers.

To gain time, the 11th company now bypasses the connecting trench, and, single file, moves out into the open.

Having gained the first crest, we descend toward the ravine. Here, as in a crucible, death-dealing explosions and fumes mingle in a hellish racket. Another hundred feet, and we are in the danger zone.

Around us, it is raining German shells. The men are silent. Their faces utterly serious, they march in step and in precise order. At the colonel's dugout, where the shells fall most heavily, a wall of fire and steel rises before us.

As I turn my head to see that my men are following me, a shell explodes, throwing a man several yards up into the air. His body comes down on the edge of a fresh crater, dead. Half a section has been thrown to the ground. I can see that they are shaken. But their morale holds in spite of their fear, and one by one they get up, and quickly and instinctively fall into line again. The man killed had been our only casualty; the danger was past. Death had entered our ranks, but it had not broken their alignment.

Led by their officers, our sections continue their advance.

"We'll give them hell," a man yells at me, laughing. "Sons of bitches, they're not going to get us."

More voices. We are giving each other courage. I smile at my men and calm them with a gesture.

"We'll sing up there. Let's go fellows." There is a feeling of satisfaction in such an assault. We're in perfect formation; it is a pleasure to defy death like that.

But beyond the crest we have passed there is another, and still no enemy trenches are to be seen.

The men are laughing.

"Another hundred yards gained, lieutenant," they shout. "Think we'll get them?"

Our battle order was admirable at that moment—marching in slow step, rifles held ready. Were the men conscious of the beauty of their movement?"

They continue to advance, looking for the enemy.

There are people who enjoy braving death. Some five hundred yards on our left, a machine gun starts firing at us. At precisely that moment, one of my men decides to give his spirits a lift by singing a café-concert hit. Soon the rest of the company is singing with him. But other machine guns now join in. It is a bad affair. I hear cries, but I decide to charge.

"Keep in line," I yell.

"Let's go," shout the men behind me. "We're winning."

And the attack continues. We reach the crest and jump into the trench. It is unoccupied; nothing but corpses.

That afternoon we spent reconnoitering. Sometimes we found empty trenches, but there also were times when we encountered the enemy where we least expected him.

At nightfall, and for thirty hours after that, we experienced a most violent bombardment. Near us, a light infantry unit was attacked with flamethrowers, but our flank was well protected. By regaining the lost crest, our assault had made it possible to establish a firm hold which would allow us to reestablish our line. Since that day, the enemy has been forced to counterattack repeatedly but fruitlessly, as the hundreds of corpses piled up before our trenches will testify. On May 20, when we returned to the Mort-Homme, the line was still unchanged.

11 FROM *Ernst Jünger*

The war also offered some quieter interludes. One of them has been described by Ernst Jünger, a German lieutenant then aged nineteen, who became a writer of great distinction. (It is taken from a book, by the way, that by no means glamorizes war, but that is full, too, of blood and shattered bones, and death.)

... On December 11 [1915], I went over the top to the advanced line, to report to Lieutenant Wetje, commanding officer of the second company, which was occupying the C sector. As I was about to jump into the trench I was startled by how it had changed during the two weeks of our absence. It had collapsed into a big trough, filled with mud a yard deep, whose occupants were splashing about it sadly like some amphibious creatures.... We poor bastards who had to do the fighting! Nearly all the trenches had fallen in, and the deep dugouts were flooded. For the next few weeks, we had to work without pause just to get a little firm ground under our feet. For the time being, I

SOURCE. Ernst Jünger, *In Strahlgewittern* (Berlin: E. S. Mittler & Sohn, 1920), pp. 27–29. Reprinted by permission of the publisher.

lodged together with lieutenants Wetje and Boje in a dugout whose ceiling, in spite of the sheet of canvas we had suspended beneath it, dripped like a watering can. . . .

One morning when, wet to the bones, I was leaving the dugout, I thought that my eyes were playing tricks on me. The battlefield, which hitherto had been marked by the solitude of death, now looked like nothing so much than a county fair. The godawful mud had driven the occupants of both lines of trenches to the parapets, and in front of the barbed wire a lively trade and exchange of liquor, cigaretts, uniform buttons and what have you was being carried on. The mass of khaki-clad figures that came out of the previously so deserted English trenches made a sight to behold.

Suddenly there was a shot from the other side. One of our fellows dropped into the mud, dead. I went to the part of our line that faced the English sap, and shouted across that I wished to speak to an officer. And indeed: some British soldiers went back, and a short while later returned with a young man who, as I could see through my field glasses, was distinguished from them by the possession of a smarter cap. At first we negotiated in English, and then, a bit more fluently, in French, while the men around us stood listening. I suggested to him that one of our people had been killed by a treacherous shot. His reply was that this had been the doing not of his company but of that next to him. "*Il y a des cochons aussi chez nous*," he said, when some shots from *our* neighboring company struck close to his head, and I got ready to take full cover very quickly. However, we kept on talking in a manner that I am tempted to say expressed a sportsmanlike respect, and in the end would have liked nothing better than to engage in an exchange of presents to mark the occasion. . . .

To know just we would stand, we solemnly declared war on each other again, to begin three minutes after the end of our parley. After a "*Guten Abend*" on his part, and an "*au revoir*" on mine, I took a shot, despite the regrets of my men, at his loophole. It was returned at once by one that almost knocked the rifle from my hands. . . .

12 FROM *Manfred von Richthofen*

This courteous an approach to war was rare, of course. And when battle was resumed, even the greatest acts of individual heroism, such as that in which lieutenant Jubert took part, or in which Jünger would, in the end usually left the lines materially unchanged. On land, World War I,—and there was no one, by the way, who had truly foreseen this in 1914—had turned into a war of machines over men, and of entrenched warfare over open movement. Yet the individual could very much affect the outcome on another front—the war's newest—the air. Ironically, it was here, in the airforce, among the men who fought with the most recent of weapons, that the ancient virtues of war survived the most clearly.

Among the air war's celebrated heroes was Germany's "red baron," Manfred Freiherr von Richthofen—the fuselages of his squadron were painted a bright vermilion—victor in some eighty engagements in the air. Here he talks about his first wound suffered in 1915.

A DROP OF BLOOD FOR THE FATHERLAND

I cannot say that I have ever been wounded. I suppose that at the critical moment, I always moved my head or pulled in my stomach. There have been quite a few times when I wondered why they never did get me. Once, a bullet made a hole through both my fur lined boots. Another time, a bullet came traveling through my muffler, and one went up my arm and came out through my fur and leather jacket, but I never got a scratch.

But then, one fine day, we started out in our big fighter plane to entertain the British with a few bombs. We reach the target, the first bomb falls. It is very interesting, of course, to find out just what effect it has had. At least you'd like to see where it hits. Unfortunately, my plane, which was fairly well equipped for hauling bombs, had the stupid characteristic of preventing one from seeing where the bomb had made contact, for after you had dropped it the moving plane would sail on over the target and hide it from view with its wings. This always annoyed me; there was no fun in it that way. It's nice to hear things go pop down below, and see the lovely grey-white cloud of the explosion, and be able to check that it's close to target. So I motioned

SOURCE. Manfred von Richthofen, *Ein Heldenleben* (Berlin: Verlag Ullstein, 1920), pp. 49–50. Reprinted by permission of the publisher.

to friend Zeumer, would he move over a little. But I forgot that this flying monster of mine had two propellers, which were spinning away to the right and left of my observer's seat. I pointed out to him where I thought the bomb had hit, and bang, my finger is caught. Surprise at first, and then I see that it's my little finger that has suffered the damage. Zeumer had not noticed a thing.

I had lost my taste for dropping bombs, unloaded what was left quickly, and headed for home.

My love for the big fighter plane, never very strong in the first place, suffered badly from this experience. I had to sit around doing nothing for a week, and was not allowed to fly. Now it just impairs my beauty, but at least I can say with pride, "I, too, was wounded in the war."

13 FROM *Sir John Monash*

Among the virtues that survived, too, was that of chivalry. Major General Sir John Monash (1865–1931), commander of an Australian division, was a witness to Richthofen's last mission.

FRANCE, 23 APRIL 1918

. . . Richthofen's Flight was seen travelling at a considerable height overhead, probably 7000 feet, and engaged a formation of our own machines consisting of R.E.8s. Some fighting took place in the air, and then suddenly one of our R.E.8s made a quick dive to within 150 feet of the ground, followed by Richthofen in a fast triplane, which rapidly overhauled our machine, and we could see him pumping tracer bullets after our machine. All the Lewis-gunners in the neighborhood immediately opened fire and made an awful row. Suddenly Richthofen's machine was seen to stagger, but recovered itself and made as if to fly off. In turning it flew directly over one of General Hobbs's batteries in the vicinity, whose Lewis-gun was

SOURCE. F. M. Cutlack, ed., *War Letters of General Monash* (London: Angus & Robertson Ltd., 1935), pp. 235–236. Reprinted by permission of the publisher and Mrs. M. M. Cutlack.

manned by the battery cook and his assistant cook. A lucky stream of bullets got the machine fair and square; it turned over, came down with a crash, and was completely wrecked.

Before the machine could be approached the enemy artillery, which, like us, had seen the aeroplane come down and had marked the spot, put down a circle of shrapnel all around it and maintained their fire for about half an hour, while Richthofen's Flight circled round overhead four or five times and then majestically flew away. Such was the requiem of this doughty and chivalrous warrior. When our people could get near the aeroplane they found that Richthofen had been shot through the head and heart by bullets, and the papers on the body left no doubt as to his identity.

Our Royal Air Force was soon on the ground; the wrecked machine and the body of Richthofen were brought in, and late in the day buried with military honours. His personal effects were afterwards taken over the German lines and dropped with a message of condolence from the Royal Air Force.

14 FROM *Sir Arthur Conan Doyle*

No romance and no chivalry, however, surrounded the other two great technical innovations of the war—poison gas and the tank. In 1915, on the Western front, the Germans pioneered the use of gas in battle. Among the observers present was the man who had invented Sherlock Holmes, but who did not invent this scene.

. . . About 5 P.M. upon Thursday, April 22 [1915], a furious artillery bombardment from Bixschoote to Langemarck began along the French lines, including the left of the Canadians, and it was reported that the Forty-fifth French Division was being heavily attacked. At the same time a phenomenon was observed which would seem to be more in place in the pages of a romance than in the record of an historian. From the base of the German trenches over a considerable

SOURCE. Sir Arthur Conan Doyle, *The British Campaign in France and Flanders 1915* (London: Hodder and Stoughton Ltd., 1917), II, pp. 46–50. Reprinted by permission of the Estate of the late Sir Arthur Canon Doyle.

length there appeared jets of whitish vapour, which gathered and swirled until they settled into a definite low cloudbank, greenish-brown below and yellow above, where it reflected the rays of the sinking sun. This ominous bank of vapour, impelled by a northern breeze, drifted swiftly across the space which separated the two lines. The French troops, staring over the top of their parapet at this curious screen which ensured them a temporary relief from fire, were observed suddenly to throw up their hands, to clutch at their throats, and to fall to the ground in the agonies of asphyxiation. Many lay where they had fallen, while their comrades, absolutely helpless against this diabolical agency, rushed madly out of the mephitic mist and made for the rear, over-running the lines of trenches behind them. Many of them never halted until they had reached Ypres, while others rushed westwards and put the canal between themselves and the enemy. The Germans, meanwhile, advanced, and took possession of the successive lines of trenches, tenanted only by the dead garrisons, whose blackened faces, contorted figures, and lips fringed with the blood and foam from their bursting lungs, showed the agonies in which they had died. Some thousands of stupefied prisoners, eight batteries of French field-guns, and four British 4.7's, which had been placed in a wood behind the French position, were the trophies won by this disgraceful victory. The British heavy guns belonged to the Second London Division, and were not deserted by their gunners until the enemy's infantry were close upon them, when the strikers were removed from the breech-blocks and the pieces abandoned. It should be added that both the young officers present, Lieuts. Sandeman and Hamilton Field, died beside their guns after the tradition of their corps.

By seven o'clock the French had left the Langemarck district, had passed over the higher ground about Pilken, and had crossed the canal towards Brielen. Under the shattering blow which they had received, a blow particularly demoralizing to African troops, with their fears of magic and the unknown, it was impossible to rally them effectually until the next day. It is to be remembered in explanation of this disorganization that it was the first experience of these poison tactics, and that the troops engaged received the gas in a very much more severe form than our own men on the right of Langemarck. For a time there was a gap five miles broad in the front of the position of the Allies, and there were many hours during which there was no substantial force between the Germans and Ypres. They wasted their time, however, in consolidating their ground, and the chance of a great *coup* passed for ever. They had sold their souls as soldiers, but the Devil's price was a poor one. Had they had a corps of cavalry ready, a pushed them through the gap, it would have been the most dangerous moment of the war. . . .

15 FROM *W. H. L. Watson*

"Would have been . . . " The conditional tense is correct. Gas warfare, despite its atrociousness, did not in fact decide, or even materially affect, the outcome of the war. For one thing, it was less than perfect technically—changing winds, for instance, sometimes drove the gas back into the attackers' lines. For another, it was another weapon that both sides could use, and did, just as both sides soon introduced some fairly effective protection against it. Consequently, hopes shifted to another technological innovation, the tank. First to develop the idea of tank warfare were the British, who thought that the new weapon might be instrumental in breaking the stalemate in the West. In this, they failed. The tank would no more decide the war than gas had. British losses were too heavy, and their reserves insufficient. Thus the Germans were given the opportunity to add tanks to their arsenal too. Still, the British came close to succeeding. Just how close may be seen from this report by a British witness, Major. W. H. L. Watson (1891–1932), on the first massive use of tanks, near Cambrai, in November 1917.

. . . Until the 17th, the enemy apparently suspected nothing at all; but on the night of the 17th–18th he raided and captured some prisoners, who fortunately knew little. He gathered from them that we were ourselves preparing a substantial raid, and he brought into the line additional companies of machine-gunners and a few extra field-guns.

The 19th came with its almost unbearable suspense. We did not know what the Germans had discovered from their prisoners. We could not believe that the attack could be really a surprise. Perhaps the enemy, unknown to us, had concentrated sufficient guns to blow us to pieces. We looked up for the German aeroplanes, which surely would fly low over the wood and discover its contents. Incredibly, nothing happened. The morning passed and the afternoon—a day was never so long—and at last it was dusk.

At 8.45 P.M. my tanks began to move cautiously out of the wood

SOURCE. W. H. L. Watson, *A Company of Tanks* (Edinburgh: William Blackwood & Sons Ltd., 1920), pp. 172–175. Reprinted by permission of the publisher.

and formed into column. At 9.30 P.M., with engines barely turning over, they glided imperceptibly and almost without noise towards the trenches. Standing in front of my own tanks, I could not hear them at two hundred yards.

By midnight we had reached our rendezvous behind the reserve trenches and below the crest of the slope. There we waited for an hour. The Colonel arrived, and took me with him to pay a final visit to the headquarters of the battalions with which we were operating. The trenches were packed with Highlanders, and it was with difficulty that we made our way through them.

Cooper led the tanks for the last half of the journey. They stopped at the support trenches, for they were early, and the men were given hot breakfast. The enemy began some shelling on the left, but no damage was done.

At 6.10 A.M. the tanks were in their allotted positions, clearly marked out by tapes which Jumbo had laid earlier in the night. . . .[1]

I was standing on the parados of a trench. The movement at my feet had ceased. The Highlanders were ready with fixed bayonets. Not a gun was firing, but there was a curious murmur in the air. To right of me and to left of me in the dim light were tanks—tanks lined up in front of the wire, tanks swinging into position, and one or two belated tanks climbing over the trenches.

I hurried back to the Colonel of the 6th Black Watch, and I was with him in his dug-out at 6.20 A.M. when the guns began. I climbed on to the parapet and looked.

In front of the wire, tanks in a ragged line were surging forward inexorably over the short down grass. Above and around them hung the blue-grey smoke of their exhausts. Each tank was followed by a bunch of Highlanders, some running forward from cover to cover, but most of them tramping steadily behind their tanks. They disappeared into the valley. To the right the tanks were moving over the crest of the shoulder of the hill. To the left there were no tanks in sight. They were already in among the enemy.

Beyond the enemy trenches the slopes, from which the German gunners might have observed the advancing tanks, were already enveloped in thick, white smoke. The smoke shells burst with a sheet of vivid red flame, pouring out blinding, suffocating clouds. It was as if flaring bonfires were burning behind a bank of white fog. Over all, innumerable aeroplanes were flying steadily to and fro.

[1] Ellipses in original.

The enemy made little reply. A solitary field-gun was endeavoring pathetically to put down a barrage. A shell would burst every few minutes on the same bay of the same trench. There were no other enemy shells that we could see. A machine-gun or two were still trained on our trenches, and an occasional vicious burst would bring the venturesome spectator scrambling down into the trench.

Odd bunches of men were making their way across what had been No-Man's Land. A few, ridiculously few, wounded were coming back. Germans, in twos and threes, elderly men for the most part, were wandering confusedly towards us without escort, putting up their hands in tragic and amazed resignation, whenever they saw a Highlander.

The news was magnificent. Our confidence had been justified. Everywhere we had overrun the first system and were pressing on.

A column of tanks, equipped with a strange apparatus, passed across our front to clear a lane through the wire for the cavalry.

On our left another column of tanks had already disappeared into the valley on their way to Flesquieres. It was Ward's company, but Ward was not with them. A chance bullet had killed him instantly at the head of his tanks. When we heard of his death later, the joy of victory died away. . . .

16 FROM *Paul von Hindenburg*

His observations were corroborated by many a witness on the other side. Thus the commanding general of Germany's armies in the field, Paul von Hindenburg (1847–1934), a man usually given to understatement, has recalled the terror caused by the British attack.

. . . As the Flanders battle was drawing to a close, a fierce conflict unexpectedly blazed up at a part of the line that had hitherto been comparatively inactive. On November 20 we were suddenly surprised by the British near Cambrai. The attack at this point was against a

SOURCE. Generalfeldmarschall von Hindenburg, *Aus meinem Leben* (Leipzig: S. Hirzel, 1920), pp. 265–267. The translation partly follows that of the English edition, *Out of My Life* (London: Cassell and Co., 1920), pp. 289–292.

portion of the Siegfried line that certainly was very strong as far as its technical construction was concerned, but that was held by few troops, and those exhausted in previous battles.

With the aid of their tanks, the enemy broke through our series of obstacles and trench lines that had been entirely undamaged. British cavalry appeared on the outskirts of Cambrai. It looked as though by the end of the year, a breach in our line would be certain after all. At this point a catastrophe was averted by the arrival of German divisions from the East, tired though these were from their long journey and from having seen too much action. Then, after a murderous defensive battle lasting several days, we succeeded in rushing in some comparatively fresh troops, taking the enemy's salient in flank by a counterattack, and almost completely restoring the original situation at a very heavy cost to the enemy. Not only the Army Headquarters Staff on the spot, but the troops themselves and our railways had performed one of the most brilliant feats of the war. . . .

The British attack at Cambrai for the first time revealed the possibilities of a major surprise attack with tanks. We had had previous experience with this weapon in the spring offensive, when it had not made any particular impression. However, the fact that the tanks had now been raised to such a pitch of technical perfection that they could cross our undamaged trenches and obstacles did not fail to have a marked effect on our troops. The physical effects of fire from machine guns and light ordnance with which the steel Colossus was provided were far less destructive than the moral effect of its camparative invulnerability. The infantryman felt that he could do practically nothing against its armored sides. As soon as the machine broke through our trench-lines, the defenders felt themselves threatened from the rear and left their posts. . . .

17 FROM *Lord Bryce*

Perhaps one other new weapon should be mentioned in addition to gas and the tank—the massive use of propaganda. Propaganda as such was anything but a recent invention. David had used it against the Pharisees, Saint Louis against the Saracens, and Joseph Chamberlain against the Boers; it is hard to think of wars in which people have not tried to convince themselves and others of the rightness of their cause and of the wrongness of that of their enemy. Still, earlier and smaller wars had usually been fought without any truly major campaigns of organized hate against the other side. World War I was different. Mass wars required mass propaganda. Thus, Austrian propaganda created an image of the Russians as rampaging barbarians, and the Russians pictured the Austrians as the perennial despoilers of the Slavs. Thus, the Germans produced a host of pamphlets, books, and drawings depicting the British—"perfidious Albion"—as a nation without Kultur, *and the tormentor of helpless Indians and Ugandans; while English propaganda specialized in converting their former German cousins into jackbooted Prussians, whose idea of relaxation consisted of raping French nurses or severing the hands of Belgian children. Lest these summaries appear to be poetic exaggerations, there follows a brief excerpt from the so-called Bryce report, a British "investigation" into supposed German war crimes in France and Belgium. The supposed inquiry was held under the chairmanship of the distinguished British historian, author of what is still one of the best books on the United States, and former ambassador to Washington. James Viscount Bryce (1838–1922). The testimony owes more to certain traditions of British pornographic literature than to observed fact, but at the time it was thought to serve its purpose. And so it did, although in some ways too well, for in the Nazi period there would be many people who felt that it was enough to have been duped once, and who refused to believe stories of German atrocities which this time were true.*

NON-COMMISSIONED OFFICER, BELGIAN ARMY

When we entered Hofstade in August last, or some village near to it, a girl of about 18 or 19 years of age complained to me and my comrades (four) that she had been violated by several German soldiers for a period of about two hours before we entered the village on the threshold of a house in full daylight and in view of villagers. She had

SOURCE. *Evidence and Documents Laid Before the Committee on Alleged German Outrages, Being an Appendix to the Report of the Committee Appointed by His Britannic Majesty's Government and Presided Over by the Right Hon. Viscount Bryce, O. M., Formerly British Ambassador at Washington* (Published by the Macmillan Company, New York, for His Majesty's Stationary Office, London, 1915), pp. 87–88. Reprinted by permission of the publisher.

been stripped of all clothing but her chemise and had bled freely from the private parts. When I saw her she was covered only with a chemise and skirt and I did not see any blood. She appeared to be very dejected and was weeping bitterly.

BELGIAN SOLDIER

I saw evidence of German atrocities between Malines and Hofstade, in a house on the high road between these two places. I saw a woman with breasts and hands cut off. The body was lying just inside the house, which was an inn. I do not know who the woman was. It was between 24th and 25th August. The Germans had been through this place the week before, but had been beaten back. There were several houses in the neighborhood. I do not know the name of the place. Everything in the inn appeared to be broken. I also saw the body of a youth, about 20. Both legs were cut off. The body was quite close to that of the woman.

BELGIAN REFUGEE

At the end of August the first engagement between the German and Belgian troops took place, and the Germans retreated. As they did so they burned all the houses in Draes-straat, Hofstade. The church, which was in the same street, was not put on fire, but the Germans shot at the windows. I saw the houses burning.

The Germans on a Tuesday morning at the end of August went into a house in the Chaussée de Tervueren, about 150 metres from the church, and put the house on fire. The inhabitants fled, and the mother of the family, a woman of about 65, was taken out of the house, and was killed by one of the German soldiers with a thrust from a lance. I saw the funeral of this woman, but I did not see the woman killed. Her son told me that his mother had been killed. I was not informed of the name of the regiment to which the German soldiers belonged.

BELGIAN SOLDIER

I was at Hofstade, the Germans were retreating, we were advancing near the headquarters of the Gendarmerie. I saw a woman about 45 years old and a boy of about 9 who had been struck with a bayonet several times, both in the face and in the body, both the boy's hands were cut off at the wrist, he was kneeling on the ground, one hand cut off was on the ground, the other hanging by a bit of skin.

SERGEANT IN BELGIAN ARMY

I was serving with my regiment at Hofstade on the 25th August. We were driving the Germans out of Hofstade. I went into a house on the left-hand side of the main road from Malines to Brussels. I there saw the body of a woman lying on the floor. Both breasts were cut off. There was also the body of a child lying close to the other body. Some of the limbs had been cut off. It was either both arms and both legs or both hands and both feet. I do not remember which. On the following day at Elewyt, a village a little further on, in a private house I saw a man and woman lying on the floor who had been bayoneted all over their bodies. The woman was dead and the man still living. I spoke to the man, who told me that the Germans had treated them so because they told a Belgian patrol that there were German soldiers in the garden.

BELGIAN SOLDIER

My company was advancing through Hofstade. In the main street is a big café. As we were passing this café we heard that a boy had been killed there by the Germans. We went in, and in one of the rooms on the ground floor was the body of a boy of about 14. The priest attached to my regiment went in with us. The village priest arrived after we got there. The boy had been bayoneted in the right side. His hands were clasped together and a bayonet had been thrust through both of them. There was a great quantity of blood about—the blood was still wet. We took the body out and put it on a stretcher. Whilst we were doing so the boy's parents came up. I did not speak to them.

BELGIAN SOLDIER

At the time of the first bombardment of Malines at Hofstade near Malines, I saw two dead men at the side of the road; they each had both hands entirely cut off. This was on the 25th Aug. I wrote down the date in my diary; we were at Hofstade. I wrote that I was at Malines all that day and went to Hofstade in the evening; we were getting some straw to sleep on and found the two bodies behind the house.

Before this, at Liège, on the 5th August, I saw a child of 8 or 9 with a bullet wound in the body—it was alive and being taken to the doctor. All my company saw this.

I saw two women and a peasant lying dead in the road at Wandre, shot.

MARRIED WOMAN

About the middle of August some German soldiers came to the town (Hofstade), and stayed there, and at first nothing was done by them. Every morning I had to supply 27 Uhlans with coffee, and some of the civilians were compelled to make trenches.

One day in August I was going to the mill to buy some flour and on the way saw a young man, 17 or 18 years old, whom I knew, lying with his two hands cut off. Blood was running from his arms and he was dying. I could not bear to remain with him, and I ran away crying. This boy worked with his father, who was a blacksmith at Hofstade, and whom I knew well by sight. I heard that the boy had attempted to run away from the Germans who were entering his house to burn it.

The Germans then ordered all the people to leave their houses at once, and I went to the bridge at Sempst. I then saw two men, father and son (aged 18), who were unarmed, and were on their way to work, shot dead by some German soldiers, who at once threw their bodies into a chalk pit. The men were bricklayers.

I then saw the Germans shoot a man, a sheep shearer, living at Sempst. I saw him a little later after the Germans had left. He then cried "Oh God! oh God!"

I ran over the bridge and took shelter in a house, which was occupied by two families, and there were 13 children in the house. One of the two men were confined to his bed with rheumatism, and the German soldiers bound this man to his bed with his hands behind his back. They then took the second man and shot him in my presence, and in the presence of all the children. I then fled. . . .

18 FROM *Alphonse Grasset*

What, though, of the miseries of war that did not need to be invented? What was the war like for the infantryman, who, whether he believed in the enemy's infamy or not, had to bear the brunt of the fighting? (And the soldier in the field, by the way, often was more immune to the excesses of propaganda than the civilian at home.) Here, the overwhelming impression is that of stark and real horror. This is so despite the gallantry, or the dedication, or the sense of excitement that even modern technology could not everywhere destroy. Horror and fear and hopelessness. In 1917, the German poet Stefan George wrote:

Most monstrous shapes of steel and iron
Escaped from their creators' hands
Laws to themselves, hurtle through space.
Grim laughter
Will be your answer if you should
Offer false tales of bygone heroes
To one who saw his brother
Who vegetated
In shamelessly raked earth like vermin
Shot into pulp and pieces.
The ancient god of battles is no more.

Two battle descriptions may stand for many. The first is by Commandant *Grasset. It is from the same book that recalled the troops' mood of departure—"sunshine cannot be reproduced on canvas"—in the early days of August 1914. Less than two weeks later, his regiment was deep in action near the Belgian border.*

. . . The sun has turned scorching hot. I look at my watch; it is not nine A.M. yet. The time seemed to pass with extraordinary slowness. The company is suffering heavily. Its action clearly is hampering the enemy, who concentrates the combined heavy fire of his infantry, artillery, and machineguns on us. We are surrounded by a heavy cloud, which for a while completely hides the battlefield from our eyes.

Dumercq has had to stop his methodical firing. I do not hear him any more.

A moment later, he shouts out to me that he is wounded. It was

SOURCE. Commandant A. Grasset, *Vingt Jours de Guerre aux Temps Héroiques* (Paris: Berger-Levrault, 1918), pp. 168–170. Reprinted by permission of the publisher.

more than that. He has received a bullet directly in the heart. It happened very simply. The death of a hero is seldom theatrical. . . .

Little Bergeyre jumps up, shouts "*Vive la France*" at the top of his voice, and falls in a heap.

Among the men lying on the ground, one could no longer tell the living from the dead. The first were entirely absorbed by their grim duties, the others lay motionless, preserving in their eternal rest the position in which death had surprised them. The wounded offer a truly impressive sight. Sometimes they will stand up, bloody and hideous, amid bursts of gunfire. They run around aimlessly, arms held out in front, eyes looking down, spinning around and around. Often they will stop and fall heavily. They have been hit by fresh bullets.

Heartrending cries, agonizing appeals, horrifying groans intermingle with the sinister howl of the projectiles. Furious contortions tell of how life is refusing to leave a strong and youthful body.

One man is trying to reattach his bloody, dangling hand to his shattered wrist. Another leaves the line holding his bowels, which, through his torn clothes, are coming out of his stomach. Soon, a bullet strikes him down.

There is no support from our artillery. Yet there are big guns in our division and in the army corps, aside from those that were destroyed on the road. Where are they? When will they come? . . . We are alone. . . .

19 FROM *Gerald Brenan*

The second eyewitness is Gerald Brenan (b. 1894), British novelist and author of several books of travel and history, among which The Spanish Labyrinth *(1943) is probably the best known. Here, he recalls some scenes from another engagement on the Western front.*

. . . The battle opened a little after sunrise on July 1, 1916, with a bombardment that shook the air with its roar and sent up the earth on the German trenches in gigantic fountains. It seemed as if no human

SOURCE. Gerald Brenan, "A Survivor's Story," in George A. Panichas, ed., *The Promise of Greatness, The War of 1914–1918* (New York: The John Day Company, Inc., 1968), pp. 44–45. Reprinted by permission of the publisher.

being could live through that. Then our men climbed by short ladders onto the parapet and began to move forward, shoulder to shoulder, one line behind the other, across the rough ground. They went slowly because each of them carried a weight of 66 pounds. A moment later the German barrage fell on our trenches, and their machine guns began to rattle furiously. Clouds of blue and gray smoke from the bursting shells, mingling with a light ground mist, hid the general view, but through the gaps I could see the little antlike figures, some of them keeping on, others falling, creeping, writhing, lying still. Each of them carried on his back a tin triangle to assist in his identification by our artillery, and the early morning sun shone on these triangles and made them glitter. But as the hours passed, I could not see that any of them had reached the German support line, and later I knew why: The Boche machine gunners had come out of their deep dugouts and were mowing them down.

All this time the barrage that had fallen on our shallow assault trenches had continued and was churning up the earth all around. As I learned later, they were still packed with troops because they had been manned in the wrong order, and two of the waves had been caught by the barrage and had never got off. Slowly the sun rose higher and higher in the sky, and the heat of that scorching day grew and grew; but I could detect no movement on the slope in front of me except that here and there a wounded man could be seen creeping toward a shell hole. It became clear that our attack had failed. Then, when darkness fell, terrible stories began to come in. They told of appalling casualties, of whole battalions reduced to thirty or forty men, and I have since read that no British Army corps had ever before suffered such losses in a single day. The pick of our young men, the first to volunteer for the war, were dead, and on our corps front not a yard had been gained.

Ten days later I was brought face to face and in the most repellent way with the consequences of this battle. My platoon was detailed for a burying party. The bodies of our men who had been mashed to pieces in the assault trenches had been brought up by night on a trench railway and bundled out onto the ground. Legs had broken off from trunks, heads came off at a touch, and nauseous liquids oozed out of the cavities. The stench was overpowering. Our job was to cut off the identity disks and bury these decomposing corpses in shallow trenches. After a few hours of this the fear of death had so entered into me that if I had been ordered to go over the top next morning I should not have been able to.

Meanwhile, as there was no more observing to be done, I had some time off. I decided to use it by looking up my friend Partridge, who was with his battalion in the new ground that had been won to the east of Albert. As, accompanied by my batman, I crossed the old front line, I seemed to be leaving a gale-swept, yet solid shore for a treacherous, chaotic region recently abandoned by the tide. The farther we went, the more desperate and confused the landscape became—shattered woods and villages, shattered trenches, abandoned equipment, and then unburied bodies. But it was also thickly populated: There was a heavy traffic of mule-drawn limbers and wagons choking the roads, and around us batteries were firing and soldiers camping by companies and battalions around their stacked rifles in open bivouacs. Then the numbers thinned out, and after a little we came to Mametz Wood, which had been the scene of heavy fighting. Its trees were torn and shattered, its leaves had turned brown, and there was a shell hole every 3 yards. This was a place where something unheard of in this war had taken place—hand-to-hand fighting in the open with bombs and bayonets. What seemed extraordinary was that all the dead bodies there lay just as they had fallen, as though they were being kept as exhibits for a war museum. Germans in their field gray uniforms, British in their khaki, lying side by side, their faces and their hands a pale waxy green, the color of a rare marble. Some of these figures still sat with their backs against a tree, and two of them stood locked together by their bayonets, which had pierced each other's bodies; they were sustained in that position by the tree trunk against which they had fallen. I felt that I was visiting a room in Madame Tussaud's Chamber of Horrors, for I could not imagine any of these corpses having ever been alive. . . .

20 FROM *Ljubomir Dabić*

Not every death occurred in battle. One that did not was that of Colonel Dimitrijević, whose own description of his role in the Sarajevo murders was cited some pages back. During the night of June 25, 1917, the executioners came to fetch him and the others condemned at Salonika from their cells. Historians are likely to continue disagreeing in their judgment on Apis—was he hero or villain,

SOURCE. Vojislav Bogićević, *Sarajevski Atentat, Izborne Stenografske Bilješke Sa Glavne Rasprave Protiv Gavrila Principa i Drugova* (Sarajevo: Arhiv Bosne i Hercegovine, formerly Državni Arhiv NRBiH, 1954), pp. 94–99. Reprinted by permission of the publisher.

creator or destroyer—as there will contine to be argument over just what the motives of the Serbian government were in staging his trial. (The argument, by the way, is among lawyers and judges as well as among historians; thus in 1953, the Supreme Court of the Federal People's Republic of Yugoslavia posthumously retried the case against Dimitrijević and associates, and found them innocent on all charges.) But there can be no argument over the manner of Dimitrijević's death, which was that of a very brave man.

This account of the condemned men's last hours was written by Lieutenant Colonel Ljubomir Dabić, of the Judge Advocate's Division of the Royal Serbian Army. Malobabić and Vulović, Black Hand members both, were involved in the Sarajevo affair along with Dimitrijević, although the precise nature of the roles they played will probably not be established with any true certainty.

After having made their confessions to arch-priest Zdranko Paunković, the condemned men Dimitrijević and Vulović gave him letters for their families; the arch-priest will pass them on today to the commanding officer. The condemned Malobabić gave him keys and combinations in order to withdraw money from a bank, which is to go to the state.

Dimitrijević, Vulović, and Malobabić were taken to the place of execution in a closed car at 1.00 A.M. [of June 26].

. . . We arrived at the place of execution at 1.30. All along the narrow path that led to it from the car Vulović talked animatedly with Lieutenant Joseph Protić [apparently a guard officer in command of the policemen who were charged with the execution]. Dimitrijević said three times: "This is a special military service we are made to perform," talking all the while with Captain Milan Stojković [apparently another officer of the guards] in a low voice. Malobabić said nothing.

At the precise spot of the execution, we had to wait for twenty minutes, the time necessary to make the preparations. It was then that Dimitrijević and Vulović asked repeatedly not to be executed before dawn, and to tell the policemen to aim well, so that they would not be massacred in the dark. This was granted. When he saw me, Dimitrijević asked if I had come on behalf of the court, and when I replied that I had, and that I was obliged to read the sentence to him, he said in a bantering tone: "Understand what has happened to me; I assure you that I am innocent."

I replied that as a man and a comrade I felt sorry to see him die in his best years, when he still could have rendered so many services to his country, but that according to the law he was guilty, and that he might find consolation in the certain knowledge that his death was necessary for the country and for public order. He seemed to be pleased to hear these words, for he said: "I beg you, tell my friends that I do not regret dying under Serbian bullets, since it is for the welfare of Greater Serbia, which I hope with all my heart will soon come about. Yes, according to the law I am guilty, and what will happen had to happen. Relations had become too strained through my fault,[1] and that is why it is necessary that I go."

Then he continued jestingly: "But why could not one have chosen a better place for the execution, preferably on a hill, from which one could have gazed at the sea. You know, what this country lacks is a bit of solemnity." His attitude was one of firmness; he was, however, quite changed, his face was pale and his voice trembled slightly. From time to time he consoled Rade Malobabić. When the latter reproached him by saying that it was due to him that he found himself in this spot, he replied: "It is fate, Rade. If you had not been with me, it would not have happened to me either. If you had stayed at Kurchumlia, you and I would have remained alive."[2]

Vulović bore himself best of all. He did not lose his sense of humor for a moment. He admitted having been guilty, but not of the crime of which he was accused. When I asked for some water while reading the sentence, and when I had drunk, he addressed me with the words: "Give me some water too, please, namesake." Taking the jug, he added: "Let's hope you don't have syphilis," to which I replied that it was too late now for such worries; he laughed in an entirely natural manner.

Malobabić was the most discouraged and beaten; he reproached himself all the time for finishing his life in this manner instead of being able to offer it freely in the cause of Serbia.

[1]The reference, presumably, is to the Serbian government, headed, as it was in 1914, by Nikola Pašić.

[2]After the outbreak of the war, Malobabić, who was an Austrian citizen, had been arrested and maltreated by the Serbian police, who apparently were unaware of the fact that he had been Dimitrijević's top espionage agent in Austria-Hungary. When Apis heard about this, he effected Malobabić's release. Kurchumlia was the place to which he took the "more dead than alive" ex-spy to recover from the effects of his prison experiences. As the Austrian advance into Serbia continued, Malobabić begged Apis not to let him fall into enemy hands, and Apis agreed that he should leave Kurchumlia, and accompany him on the Serbian retreat into Greece.

After the sentences of both courts and the orders from headquarters concerning the executions had been read, which took from 2.00 to 4.30 [A.M.], Dimitrijević and Vulović took leave from all the officers present, bidding them adieu. Dimitrijević turned to the priest and kissed his hand, and in a low voice spoke some words to Colonel Dunić [another officer detailed to attend the execution]. The three condemned men embraced, and Dimitrijević turned toward us, saying, as he put his hand on Malobabić's shoulder: "I affirm again that this man was a good patriot and that he was always acted for the welfare of Serbia."

Then the three condemned men stepped down into the ditches that had been dug for the purpose, and placed themselves in front of the stakes, Dimitrijević on the right, Vulović in the middle, and Malobabić on the left. When stepping down, Dimitrijević said: "It seems that the ditch is not quite deep enough for me." When it came to blindfolding Malobabić, and the latter asked that one dispense with it, Dimitrijević said: "Let them do it, Rade, the law requires it." After being blindfolded, Dimitrijević and Vulović cried: "Long live Greater Serbia!" and Dimitrijević added: "Long live Yugoslavia!" At the last moment, Vulović said: "Adieu, Dragutin" to Dimitrijević once again, and Dimitrijević passed on this farewell to Malobabić, adding: "Adieu, Rade," to which the latter made no reply.

Although it had taken more than two hours and a half to read the sentence, dawn had not broken yet, and the three condemned men waited calmly, talking to each other from time to time in low voices. At one point, Malobabić turned almost entirely away from us, and there was talk that he was thinking of escaping and was looking for a way to do so. However, he did no such thing. All he did was to give some more instructions concerning his property which he was leaving to his family.

The condemned Vulović threw his cane over his head from the ditch, asking that it be given to Major Alexander Savić, who should take it to his wife, and asked that his wallet be taken from his pocket.

Malobabić succumbed after the first five shots, while the two others suffered longer, twenty shots having to be fired at each of them. No one was hit in the head.

The doctor made the usual examination, and the condemned men were buried.

The execution was over on June 13/26, 1917, at 4.47 in the morning.

21 FROM *Ferdinand Foch*

It was another year and one-half before the dying was over. When it was, in November 1918, the Supreme Commander of the Allied Armies, General Foch (1851–1929), issued the following Order of the Day.

SOLDIERS OF THE ALLIED ARMIES

After having resolutely checked the enemy, you have for months, with untiring faith and energy, attacked him ceaselessly.

You have won the greatest battle in History, and saved the most sacred cause, the Liberty of the World.

Be proud!

You have pinned immortal glory to your flags.

The gratitude of posterity is yours.

F. FOCH
Marshal of France
Commander in Chief of the Allied Armies

SOURCE. Maréchal Foch, *Mémoires pour servir à l'histoire de la Guerre de 1914–1918* (Paris: Librairie Plon, 1931), II, 320.

PART THREE
The Consequences

In our present world of cold and hot wars, Versailles almost arouses nostalgia. It was at least a settlement, and one that in the best moments of the 1920s seemed a basis for slow improvement in international relations.

CRANE BRINTON, *A History of Civilization*

The Germans lost a war in 1919. We [Austrians] lost a world.
We woke up one day, and our grandparents were foreigners.

HANS WEIGEL, *O du mein Österreich*

V HISTORIANS

The war affected the course of history as few others have. It led to revolution in Russia and elsewhere. It destroyed two empires, the Austro-Hungarian and the Turkish, and greatly diminished two others, the German and the Russian. It created a large number of new nations, in Europe as well as in the Middle East. It replaced a number of monarchies with republics, many of them unstable. It signaled the end of the supremacy of Europe, and, ultimately, of colonialism. It prepared the way for fascism and for another, bloodier war.

Hardly any of these things had been either desired or expected by the powers when they went to war in 1914. The forces unloosed in the conflict were greater than any one nation's or any group of nations' power to control them. The greatest such attempt was made in the Paris peace treaties of 1919, of course, but to a large extent even these treaties merely confirmed what had taken place, such as the breakup of the Habsburg empire. Still, had the Allies shown more magnanimity and wisdom than they did (or than the Germans had when it had been their turn to dictate peace to the defeated Russians at Brest-Litovsk in early 1918), events might have taken a different course. Yet Versailles was no blindly punitive victor's peace either, as the following description of its main terms may make clear.

22 FROM *A. J. P. Taylor* *Afterwards: 1919*

Taylor (b. 1906), fellow of Magdalen College, Oxford, has written on a wide variety of topics—on German, British, Russian, Italian and Habsburg history, on diplomatic, military, and political affairs. He has often been controversial and

SOURCE. A. J. P. Taylor, *Illustrated History of the First World War* (London: George Rainbird Ltd., 1963; New York: G. P. Putnam's Sons, 1964), pp. 203–206. Reprinted by permission of the publishers.

always stimulating, though he may be at his least controversial in this passage where, while clearly taking sides (in defense of Versailles), he avoids the uncompromising partisanship that characterized much of the more immediate post-war discussion of the treaty.

. . . The Germans had expected something much more generous than the treatment of Brest-Litovsk, not much less. They had supposed that Germany, too, would be accepted as a peaceful, democratic power, once the Kaiser was got rid of and the fighting brought to an end. There would be peace without victors and vanquished. This did not happen. The Allied peoples had been told during the war that there was nothing to choose between Germans. They remembered that the German Socialists, now heading the Government, had supported the war until it ended in defeat. . . . Hence there was no such reconciliation as there had been after the Great War a century previously, when the Allies made out that they had been fighting only Napoleon, not France. It was easier for despotic monarchs to forget their hatreds than for democratic statesmen or peoples. The Germans felt that they had been cheated: first in having peace dictated to them; then in being treated as enemies.

In the last resort, after laborious months, security, reparation, justice, all tangled together. As security, Germany was disarmed: no air force, virtually no navy, no tanks, no heavy guns, and a control commission to see that this was enforced. The French wanted to limit the German army to 200,000 conscripts. The British and Americans, shocked at the very word "conscription", insisted on a limit of 100,000 long-service volunteers, who became the training officers of a new army later. The Anglo-Saxons, somewhat ashamed of this one-sided disarmament, slapped in a clause that it was designed in order to make disarmament easier for others. This clause, though not a binding promise, had awkward consequences later on. The victor Powers found themselves pushed into the Disarmament Conference. The disarmament arrangements, though often criticized later, worked while they lasted. Germany was genuinely disarmed, as near as makes no difference. The victors enjoyed fifteen years of real security. No treaty, after all, can provide that it will be enforced when those who benefit from it are too supine to enforce it.

The French were not content with the disarmament of Germany. They wished to detach the left bank of the Rhine from Germany and to set it up as an independent state, or rather as a state dependent on themselves. Among the few German protagonists of this scheme was Konrad Adenauer, the mayor of Cologne. Lloyd George[1] resisted it firmly. He looked forward to a time when men, including himself, would come to their senses, and was determined that reconciliation with Germany should not be made impossible. He was prepared to accept temporary terms of inequality: the Rhineland to be made a neutral zone and to be occupied by Allied troops for fifteen years; the Saar valley, with its coal mines, to be in French hands for the same period, to compensate for the mines in north-east France which had been wilfully wrecked by the Germans. These terms would pass. Germany would emerge free and united. A separate Rhineland would offend against the self-determination in which they all claimed to believe. Lloyd George silenced the French cry for security by proposing instead an Anglo-American guarantee of France against German aggression. Clemenceau[2] accepted the offer, only to be defrauded when the American Senate failed to ratify the treaty of guarantee. German territory in the west remained intact except for the return of Alsace and Lorraine to France, and a couple of villages added to Belgium.

On the eastern frontier of Germany, Lloyd George had a more difficult time. Wilson, or maybe Wilson's expert advisers, sympathized with the new Poland, and were lavish with what had been German territory. The French, too, were of course strong on the same side. Lloyd George, so often despised as unprincipled, was the one man who stuck to his principles. He insisted on a plebiscite in Silesia, which turned out in Germany's favor (too much so from the point of national division). He held out firmly against the incorporation into Poland of Danzig, a purely German town. Thanks to Lloyd George, Danzig became a Free City—politically independent, though economically available for Poland. Thus the arrangement which ostensibly provoked Germany into starting the Second World War was actually designed for her benefit. It is hard to find fault with the new frontiers of Germany drawn at Paris from the standpoint of self determination. This was a "fair" settlement if there can be such a thing. There was one negative offence against principle. The German

[1] David Lloyd George (1863–1945), British prime minister 1916–1922 and leader of the British delegation at Paris.

[2] Georges Clemenceau (1841–1929) French wartime premier and leading French spokesman at the peace conference.

inhabitants of rump Austria wished to join Germany now that the Habsburg Empire had vanished; and there could be no clearer case for national unification. The French objected that the war would have been fought in vain and victory would be a mockery, if Germany came out of the war with more inhabitants than when she went in. The argument was accepted. Union of Austria with Germany was forbidden except with the consent of the future League of Nations. The French argument was reasonable enough. However the Germans managed to acquire at least one Austrian without anyone's consent. He was Adolf Hitler. Perhaps it would have been better if they had acquired the other six million Austrians also.

Reparations caused most fuss during the negotiations, and came in for most blame later. It was of course absurd to expect that Germany could be made to pay all the costs of the war, though the statesmen, from Lloyd George downwards, shrank from explaining publicly how absurd it was. All the same, there was excuse for the difficulties which the statesmen got into. It seemed reasonable enough that the Germans, whose own country had not suffered at all, should repair the damage which they had caused in Belgium and northern France. This was awkward for Great Britain, which had also suffered little damage, and would therefore get little reparation. She claimed German ships, in compensation for those which the U-boats had sunk, only to discover that this put her own shipyards out of work. The idealist Smuts was ready, as usual, with a way out: he suggested that war pensions were also a civil damage, and thus the British got their share after all. The French wanted to draw up a bill for the total damage, and present it to the Germans, even though it would be beyond their capacity to pay. Wilson, on the other hand, wanted to fix Germany's capacity, which would be much less than the French claim. Lloyd George realized that any such total would be wildly inflated in the excited conditions of the time, an excitement which his own financial experts shared. He proposed that reparations should be settled in quieter days later. He got his way. Germany had to recognize full liability—the so-called "war guilt" clause; her actual payments were left to an expert commission. Nothing caused so much ill-feeling in the inter-war years as the wrangles over reparations. Yet the question had been left open in the interests of reconciliation and good sense. Unfortunately, these took longer to operate than Lloyd George had hoped; and when they did they were out of date. . . .

23 FROM *René Albrecht-Carrié* *Economic Consequences*

What went beyond the rights and wrongs of Versailles, and of its companion treaties with the other defeated nations, was the larger issue of the decline in European power, which affected victors and vanquished alike. Some of the larger economic and political reasons for it are analyzed by an American historian of note. Albrecht-Carrié (b. 1904) professor of history at Barnard College and at Columbia's School of International Affairs, also has written extensively on nineteenth century diplomatic history.

Only the passage of time could assuage and soften exacerbated national feelings. Time likewise would be needed to make good the physical damage of war, which no arrangement of peace could of itself undo. Before 1914 there had existed a world-encompassing network of economic and financial relations. Stable currencies, trade balances, international exchanges of capital and goods had gradually developed in the midst of an expanding world economy, and they had largely come to be taken for granted. These exchanges, like individual travel, had been essentially free, unhampered by any appreciable degree of governmental interference.

To this state of affairs the war had brutally put an end, and mention has been made of the inevitable extension among all the principal belligerents of the functions and powers of the state. Just as war was considered unfortunate and its recurrence to be prevented, so there was after the war a widespread expectation that peace would bring a return to normality, meaning prewar conditions. Much of this hope was rooted in illusion, as the subsequent course of events would painfully establish, the same sort of illusion that tended to equate the cessation of fighting with the restoration of peace.

The single word that sums up best the economic effects of the war is *dislocation*, and there was no reason to assume that the scattered fragments would be put back together in their old pattern. Because of their own war demands, the European states had been unable to

SOURCE. René Albrecht-Carrié, *The Meaning of the First World War* (Englewood Cliffs: Prentice-Hall, Inc., 1965), pp. 110–113, 140–146. Reprinted by permission of the publisher.

supply their foreign markets with the usual goods. Their place had been taken by others, most of all by the United States, to the expansion of whose industry and agriculture the war had given a great boost. The American manufacturer had no desire to relinquish a profitable market to its former suppliers merely because they had been such; why should he, under a regime of free competition? To a considerable extent the industrial plant of Europe was run down—some of it, as in France, wholly destroyed—and agricultural production was appreciably affected by the shortage of fertilizers.

There was everywhere a crying need for reconstruction, in the effecting of which the state had to assume a large role. The French case is a good illustration, especially because of the political and international complications that grew out of it. The view that the war had been a national undertaking was wholly fair, from which it followed that the consequent damage, be it human or material, was a proper charge on the nation. In France, as elsewhere, the state assumed the burden of war pensions. But the loser of property, the owner of a destroyed factory in the war zone, was likewise and with similar fairness compensated. The burden of these obligations mounted to astronomical proportions, certainly by comparison with what had been normal pre-1914 budgets.

This burden came on top of the financing of the war itself, and that too had far exceeded the expectations and what were thought to be the capabilities of pre-1914 economies. There was no outright bankruptcy in 1919, but all the belligerents emerged from the war with enormously inflated national debts, the British some tenfold, the German by a factor of forty. From the beginning, gold payments had been suspended and currencies had begun to fluctuate. While the war lasted there was cooperation among the Allies, and then with the United States, in controlling currency relations, but the pressure for a return to free economies caused the removal of controls and gave full scope to the manifestation of the effects of inflation.

The international aspect of finance was most troublesome. Foreign debts had been a normal component of the prewar international scene, one that was properly integrated into the network of international trade. The Central Powers had been largely cut off from foreign sources of capital, hence they had to rely on internal borrowing, but the American capital market was open to the Allies, of which they made full use. The difficulties they were about to encounter in continuing this practice were removed as a consequence of the

American intervention. But in the First World War the view did not prevail, as it did in the Second, that the war was a common enterprise to which all should contribute according to their means. That brilliant invention, Lend Lease, was largely a product of the lessons of the First World War. In the earlier war America contributed unstintingly, but in the form of loans, to which further ones were added after the termination of hostilities for the purpose of reconstruction.[1]

The result, not the least important effect of the war, was to reverse the position of the United States from that of debtor to one of wellnigh universal creditor. The source of difficulty lay in the abruptness of the reversal, which had not grown out of a gradual readjustment of economic relationships but very suddenly out of the wealth-destroying fact of war. The significance of the transformation was little understood at first, not least in the United States where the need of understanding was greatest. Even after some years had passed an American President could sum up his view of the matter in the simplist comment, "Well, they hired the money!" This unexceptionable expression of New England moral rectitude in money matters was not so much wrong as it was irrelevant. For it was based on denial or ignorance of economic reality. The discharge of international financial obligations is inextricably tied to the balance of trade. Before the war it had been the proper thing for America to have a favorable balance of trade and be a debtor nation, just as the reverse was the proper condition for Britain. But the war reversed the debtor position of the United States while emphasizing more than ever her favorable balance of trade. It is not easy to see how America, by a deliberate act, could have in turn reversed the balance of trade, though she might have avoided aggravating the situation. The Fordney-McCumber Tariff Act of 1922 was not so much an expression of graspingness, let alone of moral wickedness, as of deficient economic thinking. But the problem remained, for which a near monopoly of the world's gold, stored under the ground, could be no permanent solution. No other solution was found, unless one can call default and abandonment a solution, and the problem is still with us, though we now have at least some understanding of the issue and as a consequence no longer seek to deal with it in moral terms. But

[1]The large debts owed the United States became a very troublesome issue after the war. The discharge of these obligations, in economic terms, constituted a problem of precisely the same nature as that of the payment of German reparations.

this is not the place to enter a discussion of the dreary record of international postwar financial relations; the intention is no more than to point out one aspect of the dislocation consequent on the war. Certainly the expectation that these things would take care of themselves once normality had been re-established was one of the more fanciful illusions of the immediate postwar period. . . .

THE EUROPEAN AFTERMATH

To be sure, the feeling also existed among the European belligerents that a return to normality meant a return to the prewar situation. But Europe had been shaken by the war in a manner that America had not; from the European standpoint the Second World War is not so much the real and great break with the past as it is a completion of unfinished business that the first war left in its train. However strong the wish to return to the past—a wish, for that matter, that many did not share—clearly too much had happened that, in contrast with the American experience, it was impossible to ignore or deny.

Though for some time we have been hearing much on the subject of the current revival of Europe—a reality, yet a still-uncertain accomplishment—stress should rather be put on Europe's loss of place in the world, her demotion. Again, to American eyes the turning point seems to be the Second World War, when the collapse of France in 1940 may be cited as the single event that most sharply startled the American consciousness. By the time Germany had been destroyed, even physically in considerable measure, and it had become clear that Britain was limping instead of having recovered her position, it is not very surprising that the feeling should have been widespread that there was little left in Europe.

This picture has validity for the period that immediately followed the Second World War, but the real turning point for Europe had actually occurred a quarter of a century before. The half-century encompassed by the Franco-Prussian War and the First World War has been characterized as the Apogee of Europe. By 1914, with the qualifications of America and Japan, Europe was truly mistress of the planet and the center that furnished the motive power of its functioning, be it in terms of crude power and political control or in terms of commerce, institutions, and ideas. The effect of the war on this situation will most conveniently be examined under two heads: first, Europe in Europe, then Europe in the wider world.

Europe was a collection of long-established entities and contained five of the world's great powers. Whatever unity there was in Europe in 1914 lay in the heritage of common culture. Real and important as this was, in the domain of power the stress was on rivalry and competition rather than unity. If there was general agreement among Europeans in the consciousness of their superiority and in the consequent legitimacy of ruling most of the rest of the world, Europe maintained at home an uneasy peace resting on a delicate balance of power. What happened in 1914 was a break in the equilibrium, but this had happened before, and it has been explained that for some time the feeling continued to prevail that the war would effect some inner readjustments but would not otherwise materially change the fundamentals of the European system in Europe, or the position of Europe in the world as a whole. The war had precisely the effect of altering radically both conditions.

So long as kings were divinely appointed rulers, defeat in war did not necessarily impair the constitutional standing of a monarchical regime. But in the twentieth century even a Russian tsar could not withstand the disgruntlement of his subjects. Four ancient dynasties were destroyed by the war: the Romanovs, the Habsburgs, the Hohenzollerns, and the Osmanlis. But startling and significant as this may have been in itself, it was less so than the destruction of a state. The Ottoman may be regarded as a somewhat special case, owing to the role of Europe's imperial urge in it, but there had been no thought at first that Austria-Hungary, one of the components of the community of major powers, would simply be no longer. The unprecedentedly radical application of the democratic principle of self-determination had produced that outcome. Danubia was a problem indeed after its fragmentation, but there was little power in the separate fragments of Danubia.

This same principle of self-determination was responsible for an extensive Russian retreat and for some appreciable German losses. Unlike the Dual Monarchy, however, Russia and Germany remained as large and recognizable entities. But for the moment, and for some indefinite future, there would be no power in either of these states. Power was all in the hands of the victors, which, among major powers, meant Britain, France, and Italy. This imbalance alone was serious enough, but even the victorious coalition was riven by inner stresses and dissents. For Italy, the strain of the war combined with the destruction of the former European balance had the effect of making that country count for even less in European affairs than her intrinsic strength may have warranted. Disgruntled and restless, like America seeking domestic and foreign scapegoats, Italy adopted a policy of retreat and retrenchment and played a role of self-effacement.

This left Britain and France. It is conceivable that an Anglo-Franco-American combination, endowed with the power and the stabilizing influence of America, might have led Europe back to a situation where the defeated, Germany and Russia, could have been reintegrated into the larger community, and thus at least have avoided some of the stresses that their exclusion created. It certainly would be more difficult, though perhaps not wholly impossible, for Britain and France, together but without America, to lead Europe back to some orderly functioning. For Britain and France to fall out would, under the circumstances, be to court suicide. Yet that is precisely what they did.

. . . [Besides], Britain and France, the former less obviously than the latter, had for some time been powers in positions of relative decline—this was the very fact which had brought them together before 1914—and they had won the war, but not alone, while the effort involved had in some ways injured them even more, France especially, than the hurt of defeat had injured a more vigorous Germany. We are dealing with one of Bismarck's imponderables, the factor of morale, will, or spirit. The fact is that neither Britain nor France was possessed of adequate power, including will, to effect an adequate reorganization of Europe. Thus victory itself was in some ways their greatest defeat. The fact that it served to conceal for a time the true reality of things was one of the aspects of the tragedy that the war had been for Europe. . . .

24 FROM *Raymond J. Sontag* *Between the Wars*

The weakness of the major powers might have mattered less had the new states that emerged been strong, united, and vital. They were not. Nor could they have been, since the war had done little to solve the major, and universal, twentieth-

SOURCE. Raymond J. Sontag, "Between the Wars," *Pacific Historical Review*, Vol 29, No. 1 (February 1960), pp. 3–8. Reprinted by permission of the University of California Press and the author.

century problems of nationalism and social unrest. In this selection Raymond J. Sontag examines some of the war's lasting domestic repercussions. Sontag (b. 1897) taught first at Princeton and then for many years at the University of California at Berkeley, where he was Ehrman professor of history. His main field has been diplomatic history, especially Anglo-German relations, and he was American editor-in-chief of the German foreign ministry archives. Historians, as this collection, too, may have illustrated, have a way of disagreeing with each other (this is one of the virtues of the profession), but there has been remarkably little argument over the magnitude of Raymond Sontag's contribution to historiography, both as a scholar and as a teacher.

. . . The war did not dispose of the problems raised by technology and nationalism. During the war the dizzy pace of scientific and technological change quickened. In pure science it is enough to recall that Einstein's general theory of relativity was completed during the war, and that the first experimental proof of the theory was afforded by observations of the deflection of light during the solar eclipse of May 29, 1919, a date which surely ranks in importance with the other crucial events of that spring—the Treaty of Versailles, the establishment of the Third International, and the formation of the Fascist party in Italy. Soon Einstein's gentle face had become familiar to a world which had not the faintest notion of the meaning of his theory.

In technology, war needs had speeded the development of the internal combustion engine, of electronics, and of chemistry. The basis had been laid for the boom in automobiles, the radio, electrical refrigeration, synthetics, motion pictures, all of the characteristic industries of the interwar years. In themselves the new or astronomically enlarged industries were to create many economic problems, bringing prosperity here, casting a blight there. In other obvious ways the war had dislocated the economic life of the world. Once the shortage of consumer goods had been overcome, the Europeans found that while they had been concentrating on war production, industry had taken root in other parts of the world, and the prewar pattern of industry and commerce was impossible to restore. Domestic and international finance were distorted by colossal governmental and intergovernmental debts, further complicated by the reparation clauses of the peace treaties.

More subtly, old financial habits had been altered by the war. Governments, fearful of taxpayers, continued to rely on loans, with fatal consequences for the currency stability which had made possible the intricate network of international finance before the war. More important, unstable currencies bred social and political instability, catastrophic in Germany, chronic in France. Even currency stabilization at too high a level, as in the twenties in Britain, could press dangerously on the social structure.

Again, the war, while ruining the fortunes of some, had made the fortunes of others. Stanley Baldwin's remark to Keynes on the House of Commons elected in 1918—"They are a lot of hard-faced men, who look as if they had done very well out of the war"[1]—could have been repeated for most of the belligerent and the neutral nations. The shady business ethics which brought quick returns during the war were equally effective in the unstable days of peace, intensified the instability, and spread to poison all ethics, public and private.

Even the most honest and clear-sighted, however, found it hard to get a foothold in the swiftly shifting economic life of the postwar years. Economists might argue that all would be well if Europe would cease to believe "political myths" and concentrate on "economic realities," but political and economic life had never been separable; both were now changing in ways which made the principles of the classical economists ever more difficult to apply to concrete situations. Only slowly was it recognized that a return to the relatively self-regulating economy of the world before 1914 was impossible. More and more, control of the economy was taken into the hands of the state; what had seemed, and indeed was in the totalitarian states, the death of freedom, was now coming to seem the safeguard of freedom in the democratic West.

At the outbreak of war in 1914, social strife had been stilled in Europe. Some optimistically hoped that cooperation in a common cause would result in permanent social peace, but most recognized that this was a truce. As the war dragged on the truce wore thin everywhere, but in Russia alone was there social revolution. Even in Russia, so far as can be told from the elections for the Constituent Assembly in November, 1917, the great majority of the Russian people had no desire for bolshevism. But of the reality of the desire for social revolution, and in particular of the determination of the peasants to lay hands on the great estates, there can be no doubt. To

[1]The remark is in J. M. Keynes, *The Economic Consequences of the Peace* (New York, 1920), 145; Baldwin is identified as the author in R. F. Harrod, *Life of John Maynard Keynes* (New York, 1951), 266.

the west and south of Russia also there was a revolution in land tenure, a revolution which proved, for the most part, of doubtful economic gain to the peasant and very rarely gave the peasant enduring social or political power.

To the West, immediately after the war, it seemed that rapid social change was possible without revolution, without even the tension of the years just before 1914. Perhaps this hope was highest in Germany, where cooperation had begun during the war between the Social Democrats, the Catholic Center, and what became the Democratic party—an alliance of workers, peasants, and the middle classes which, if it endured, could easily control policy. In the elections of January, 1919, this "Weimar Coalition" won over three-quarters of the votes. In the election of June, 1920, the coalition was reduced to a minority in the Reichstag, and it was never again to become a majority. Anger at the Treaty of Versailles helps to explain this shift, but in 1920 and later a coalition of center and left would have had a majority if the left had not been split. Standing aloof were the Independent Socialists and the Communists. The Independent Socialists party soon disintegrated, but to the end of the Weimar Republic the Communists were the unremitting enemies of the non-communist left. In these first years, the Communists would have been happy to make a tactical alliance with the Socialists, just as they offered their "support" to the British Labor party. But the nature of that support was clearly and publicly stated by Lenin in his orders to the British Communists. They were to support the Labor party "in the same way as a rope supports the hanged." On this basis, the Labor party, like the German Social Democrats, refused to be supported. The result in Germany was opposition and harrassment until, in the last agony of the Weimar Republic, Communists and Nazis cooperated in a political strike. Elsewhere there were the same wrecking tactics: in France and Italy both the Socialist party and the trade union movement were split.

The results of the wrecking tactics of the Comintern varied from country to country. Only in Germany were the fatal results clear. In Britain the direct result on Labor party solidarity was negligible. But even in Britain, first the Coalition government and then the Conservative party sought assiduously to identify the Labor party with bolshevism; the Zinoview Letter is merely the most dramatic episode in a continuing campaign. In France the 1919 poster of the ferocious Bolshevik with the knife between his teeth was the beginning of a campaign to identify the left with treason, a campaign which went on to and beyond the outbreak of war in 1939. In Italy opposition to communism was the most effective part of the fascist program. In eastern and southeastern Europe, fear of communism was exploited to justify violent repression of all political and social discontent. Nowhere was there the possibility of a communist seizure of power. Everywhere fear of communism was an effective weapon against the noncommunist left, and social reform. Everywhere the split on the left weakened the advocates of social change, and drove the timid and gullible into alliance with the opponents of change.

At this point technological change and its offspring, social unrest, merge with the evolution of nationalism in the years between the wars. Partly as a result of Allied promises of self-determination, partly because of the privations of the war, partly because of the lessened or broken power of the European belligerents, the demand for national unity and independence spread over the globe. Outside Europe, where there was a native leader to direct the nationalist movement, like Mustapha Kemal in Turkey, Zaghlul in Egypt, Gandhi in India, or Sun Yat-sen in China, the revolt against European domination attained complete or partial success. Everywhere imperialism was on the defensive; the days when the world was an extension of Europe were over. Aside from the conspicuous exception of Turkey, however, native nationalism rarely meant an increase in either economic or political stability.

Still less did self-determination in Europe fulfill the hopes of the war years. In eastern and southeastern Europe, from Finland to Greece, there now stretched thirteen states with a population totalling over one hundred million, all created or greatly changed by the war. They varied in size and in political and social strength. Nearly all in the early postwar years had democratic constitutions modelled after those of the victorious western democracies; nearly all sooner or later became dictatorships, open or veiled, benevolent or oppressive. Nearly all lived increasingly in fear, fear of each other, fear of Germany, Russia, or Italy, fear of internal upheaval. . . .

The experience of states so various cannot, of course, be brought under a single generalization. A state like Czechoslovakia, blessed with rich and varied resources, a highly trained bureaucracy, and statesmen like Masaryk and Beneš, cannot be equated with an impoverished peasant state like Bulgaria, or a state like Jugoslavia where the very existence of national feeling was in doubt. Taken as a whole, however, the rulers of the states of eastern and southeastern Europe relied increasingly on a violent, intolerant nationalism to gain and maintain their power and to prevent, not merely social revolution, but social change.

In the end the dominant social groups in Italy made the same choice. Right up to the end the march on Rome could have been prevented if there had been a firm will to resist Mussolini. It was the will which was lacking. After the war the parliamentary game, perfected over two generations by Italian politicians, was no longer workable. The circumstances of Italy's entrance into the war, the sorry conduct of the war, and indignation at the minor role assigned to Italy at the peace conference had discredited the old parliamentary leaders. . . .

In retrospect it is less hard to understand why Germany took the same path than why the Weimar Republic lasted so long. Certainly the results of the war were a greater affront to German national spirit and the social consequences of postwar economic instability were more demoralizing. Undoubtedly the Republic survived partly because of the disciplined strength of the German labor movement, demonstrated at the time of the Kapp Putsch in 1920, and partly because of fear that, if there were a nationalist revolution, the name of Germany might, as General Groener bluntly warned in 1919, disappear from the map. Certainly, however, credit must be given to a few statesmen, and particularly Stresemann, who had a program and were willing to fight for it. By 1933 Stresemann was dead, the strength of the labor unions had been drained by the depression, and fear of French intervention had waned. As in Italy the triumph of the Nazis could have been prevented by the use of force, but, with no clear notion of what there was to fight for, the will to resist had collapsed. . . .

What this analysis suggests is that the economic instability of the years after 1914 pressed with crushing weight on the political and social structure of every European state. . . .

25 FROM *Gordon A. Craig* *The Revolution in War and Diplomacy*

It also acted as a crushing weight on the conduct of international affairs. Gordon Craig—like Sontag and Albrecht-Carrié, less sanguine about the effects of the war than A. J. P. Taylor—has examined the potentially murderous changes that appeared in post-1918 Europe. Gordon Craig (b. 1913), Sterling professor of history at Stanford, is a man of many talents, equally at home in military, political, diplomatic, and cultural history. His Politics of the Prussian Army, 1640–1945, *which remains the basic work on that topic, probably is the best known of his books, but he has written with equal authority and style on German statecraft from Bismarck to Adenauer, on the battle of Königgrätz, on postwar diplomacy, on German nineteenth century literature, and on a variety of other topics.*

. . . Before it was over, the war had wrought changes in almost every aspect of Western society—its structure, its institutions, its values—and it is possible that, if we look at those changes with the benefit of fifty years of hindsight, we may succeed in throwing a little light upon some of our present perplexities. These pages will attempt to deal with the effects of the 1914 conflict on two of the most important institutions of the Western world—war itself and diplomacy.

It is appropriate that these two be considered together, for they belong together. Classically, diplomacy was—in Sir Ernest Satow's definition—the process of employing tact and intelligence in the adjustment of the relations and the interests of independent states, and war was the means used for the same purpose when tact and intelligence failed. As the great German military theorist Clausewitz once explained, war was not an independent and self-sufficient, agency, but merely a continuation of policy by other means. It was an instrument of statecraft, its ends and even its means determined by the requirements of policy, and its results defined and legalized by diplomatic negotiation.

The greatest statesmen of the nineteenth century understood this intimate relationship. At the time of Prussia's mobilization against

SOURCE. Jack J. Roth, ed., *World War I: A Turning Point in Modern History* (New York: Roosevelt University, 1967), pp. 9–24. Reprinted by permission of Alfred A. Knopf, Inc.

France in July, 1870, for example, Bismarck read and underscored the phrase "Blessed are the peacemakers!" on his devotional wall calendar. This has sometimes been taken as a proof of the chancellor's essential cynicism; it might more properly be interpreted as a sign of determination on his part that the impending war would be kept within its political bounds and would be ended by diplomatic means as quickly as was expedient, once the state's political objectives had been secured. This kind of politico-military coordination was not always easy to achieve, and Bismarck himself had serious difficulties with the Prussian Chief of Staff during the last phase of the French war. But even so, despite the friction that occurred in concrete cases, there was, until 1914, fairly general agreement that the tasks of the soldier and the statesman (or diplomat) were complementary.

Perhaps the most fateful change effected by the First World War was the destruction of this relationship. Warfare was revolutionized in a way that made it increasingly difficult for civilian authorities to control. Simultaneously, the expanding violence of the conflict smashed the very framework of traditional diplomacy and released forces which, in the subsequent period, militated against the kind of consensus necessary to effective international collaboration and undermined the authority and prestige of professional diplomats in their own countries.

I

When we talk of the revolution that has taken place in warfare in our time, we think first of the frightening ways in which science and technology have enhanced its potential for destruction. This process, which culminated (or perhaps merely reached its penultimate stage of dreadfulness) in the Second World War, began during the first, and did so with a suddenness that startled the soldiers themselves. After one of the first British attacks in Flanders, a young subaltern said to Lieutenant General Sir Douglas Haig, "Sorry, sir. We didn't know it would be like that. We'll do better next time." The remark was prompted by the ghastly experience of learning for the first time what the combination of well-placed machine guns and barbed wire could do to massed attacks across an open field. Similar excuses must have been made on other occasions by regular officers of the armed forces—by Austrian commanders on the Drina and Galician fronts in 1914, for example, or by Russian officers on the Gorlice-Tarnow line in 1915—for those who had made a career of soldiering before 1914 always seemed to be more surprised than the non-professionals by the forms their vocation took during the First World War. Conventional assumptions about strategy and tactics were repeatedly shattered by the appearance of new weapons, or combinations of weapons, or techniques of combat. Neither the machine gun nor the use of wire was new in 1914, but their combination in articulated defensive systems and scientifically devised patterns of fire was new enough to have escaped the attention of those who made war plans, and this had a decisive effect upon the tactics of the war. Nor was this combination the only innovation. Others were the Big Bertha gun, the use of the submarine on a massive scale, the employment of smoke and poison gas to screen infantry attacks, the use of manned aircraft for reconnaissance, for anti-troop and anti-air combat, and for the bombing of installations, and the introduction of the tank. And this list is not exhaustive.

In the use of these weapons the armies of 1914–1918 were not always expert, and the results were sometimes modest. Only about 1,400 Englishmen and 750 Germans lost their lives as a result of air raids between 1914 and 1918 (a far cry from the 75,358 homes and residential buildings totally destroyed and the 135,000 persons who were killed in fourteen hours of aerial bombardment of Dresden in 1945). Poison gas proved an unpredictable weapon that was likely to kill as many friends as foes; the tank was misused in its first appearance in the field and played no important role until the war was almost over. Even so, the new weapons had come to stay; as time passed, they would be improved, and eventually they would be superseded by far more effective ones. There were people in the period after 1918 who tried to pretend that this was not so, and who sought to block new expenditure on armor or new experimentation with air power; but these were people who failed to draw the proper conclusions from the first worldwide conflict.

In a technical sense, the First World War, as Hanson Baldwin has written, "provided a preview of the Pandora's box of evils that the linkage of science with industry in the service of war was to mean." It started that *Technisierung* of war which engrosses so much of the energies and resources of modern nations, and makes the average citizen so apprehensive of "missile gaps" and "technological breakthroughs" and other presumed threats to his security that he is apt to give uncritical support to his nation's armed establishment.

Important as this change in the nature of warfare was, it was less revolutionary than another: the extent to which war now absorbed the full energies of the societies that engaged in it. The war of 1914 was the first total war in history, in the sense that very few people living in the belligerent countries were permitted to remain unaffected by it during its course. This had not been true in the past. Even during the great wars against Napoleon many people could go on living as if the world were at peace. All of Jane Austen's characters did so; none of them ever mentions the campaigns on the continent at all. It is said that on the evening of the allied disaster at Austerlitz there was great excitement in London, caused not by the military defeat, but rather by a boxing match between two well-known champions. This kind of detachment, which was true also of the wars in Central Europe in the 1860s, was wholly impossible during World War I. This was, for one thing, the first war in which the distinction between soldier and civilian broke down, a development that was partly due to the expansion of warfare made possible by those technological innovations already mentioned. When dirigibles began to drop bombs over London and submarines began to sink merchant ships, war had invaded the civilian sphere and the battle line was everywhere.

But this relative universalizing of the possibility of death in battle was not the only thing that made war total. Even when the dirigibles did not come, the civilian was caught up in the war and all of his activities were geared to its requirements. Once it had been discovered, in the winter of 1914, that the war was not going to be over by Christmas, that it was not going to be a short war like those of 1866 and 1870, and that it was not going to be won by military means alone but by the effective mobilization of the total resources of the nation and its allies, every mature citizen became an active participant in the war effort. He was subjected to disciplines and deprivations similar to those binding on the soldiers at the front, restrictions upon his freedom which varied with the fortunes of war and the distance of his country from the theater of operations. The energy and morale of the civilian now became just as important a resource as the spirit and determination of the man in the trenches—which, of course, is why the enemy tried to drop bombs on him or starve him into compliance with its will.

Moreover—and here we come to the most fateful aspect of these changes—precisely because war became so total and was so prolonged, it also became ideological, taking on a religious cast that had not characterized warfare in the West since the Thirty Years' War. Front-line soldiers could feel sympathy for fighting men on the other side who had to put up with the same dangers and miseries that they bore themselves; and, on holidays, they could even declare private armistices with them and exchange presents. Aviators, with a chivalry that belonged to older forms of war, were known to drop wreaths on the graves of enemy fliers or—as in the case of the German ace Richthofen, who was shot down behind French lines—to give them elaborate funerals. The civilian was not given to this kind of behavior. He could not look the enemy in the face and recognize him as another man; he knew only that it was "the enemy," an impersonal, generalized concept, that was depriving him of the pleasures of peace. As his own discomfort grew, his irritation hardened into a hatred that was often encouraged by government propagandists who believed that this was the best way of maintaining civilian morale. Before long, therefore, the enemy was considered to be capable of any enormity and, since this was true, any idea of compromise with him became intolerable. The foe must be beaten to his knees, no matter what this might cost in effort and blood; he must be made to surrender unconditionally; he must be punished with peace terms that would keep him in permanent subjection.

The result of this was that the cautionary precept of Clausewitz was ignored and that rational calculation of risk versus gain, of compromise through negotiation versus *guerre à outrance*, became virtually impossible for the belligerent governments. There were soldiers and statesmen during the First World War who understood the truth later expressed by Professor Herbert Butterfield, when he wrote, after the second world conflict:

"If you possess an international order, or if it is your desire to assert the existence or the authority of such an order, you are the party which must refrain from conceiving the ends of war as though you were fighting barbarian hordes entirely outside the system. . . . So long as an international order exists, or so long as we may desire one to exist, wars must come short of the last degree of irreconcilability and must retain some of the characteristics of a conflict between potential allies, some trace of the fact that they are quarrels between friends."

Unfortunately, those who felt this way were few and ineffective. As the war expanded in scope and violence, the masses who had to bear its rigors closed their minds to reason and called for a war of extermination.

It is sometimes pointed out, as a proof of the power of special interest groups in the determination of Germany's wartime policy, that both Chancellor Theobald von Bethmann Hollweg and Foreign Minister Richard von Kühlmann were forced out of office because they advocated a peace short of total victory. It is true that these officials were the victims of a military–big-business cabal that did not want a negotiated settlement, but it is surely worth noting that their dismissal elicited not the slightest evidence of any popular indignation over the treatment accorded them. Nor should it be forgotten that, when former Foreign Secretary Lord Lansdowne, sickened by the slaughter in the trenches, wrote a letter to the *Daily Telegraph* in November, 1917, in which he urged that a negotiated peace be arranged while there was still something of European civilization to save, he was viciously attacked by the Northcliffe and Rothermere press, denounced by politicians who described his letter as "craven" and "inept," and—in the words of his biographer—subjected to "a flood of invective and an incredible mass of abusive correspondence which, though largely incoherent, was marked by a violence rare in English political life."

In the First World War, popular passion was probably more responsible than governmental obtuseness, not only for the prolongation of the war to the point where the old framework of Europe was smashed beyond repair, but also for the worst of the mistakes made at the peace conference as well. It is easy to understand why Jan Smuts of South Africa, watching war-induced hatreds prevail over reason at Paris, should have been moved to tell his friend John Maynard Keynes the story of the old Griqua chief, who, in perilous times, prayed: "Lord, save Thy people. Lord, we are lost unless Thou savest us. Lord, this is no work for children. It is not enough this time to send Thy son. Lord, Thou must come Thyself."

As a result of the First World War, therefore, the art of warfare had been revolutionized by technological innovation, extended in scope, and given a pseudo-religious cast—and for all of these reasons it had become more dangerous, more destructive, and much more difficult to get back under control once it had been loosed.

II

The changes wrought by the war in diplomacy were equally profound and were rooted in the tendency of warfare to assume its absolute and most unrestrained forms by 1917 and 1918.

In the first place, as has already been indicated, the very context within which diplomats had operated in the past was altered out of recognition by the prolongation of the war. The nineteenth-century diplomatic system—Europe-centered and dominated by five self-confident and, for the most part, monarchical powers—dissolved in a holocaust unparalleled in history. The Habsburgs, the Hohenzollerns, and the Romanovs now left the stage of history, and out of their empires the peace-makers in Paris fashioned new states that entered the diplomatic community without either tradition or experience to guide them. The war also loosened the ties of empire, inspiring the British dominions to demand a stronger voice in the determination of imperial policy and arousing a desire for full sovereignty and independence in foreign affairs among the dependencies and protectorates of all colonial powers. Even during the course of the war, it had become apparent—with the intervention of Japan and the United States—that Mazzini's description of Europe as the lever that moved the world was no longer a true one, and that the course of world affairs could no longer be determined by congresses or ambassadorial conferences like those of Berlin and Algeciras. With the sharp increase in the number of geographically diverse states participating in world affairs—a tendency accelerated by the Second World War—new forms of diplomatic organization had to be found; the League of Nations was only the first of the attempts made since 1919 to cope with this problem.

The expansion of the diplomatic community was not the only change. Equally disturbing in its effects was the breakdown of intellectual homogeneity of the diplomatic system. Before 1914, the states which were active in international affairs were in general agreement about basic things. As Charles Burton Marshal has written:

> "Their regimes drew on a generally common fund of history. The frame of discourse among them was unified to a degree permitting any government participating significantly in world affairs to be confident of having its utterances understood by others in the sense intended. None was a revolutionary power. Ideologies were "a minor theme" through most of the period. . . . The basis of general order was not at issue. A common notion of legitimacy prevailed."

After 1918, all that was changed. The nations no longer accepted the same norms of international behavior, and it was often true that their representatives used the same words in ways quite different from their colleagues from other lands.

The fact that the war ended, on one hand, in revolution and, on the other, with a punitive peace settlement made this almost inevitable. In the first flush of their victory, the new regime in Russia, for example, made their rejection of all of the principles of the old diplomacy explicit, and Lenin and Trotsky earnestly attempted to abolish what they considered a wicked bourgeois institution that was wholly inappropriate for a proletarian state. When this attempt failed and they were forced in self-defense to cultivate contacts with other powers through traditional channels, and even to seek admittance to organizations like the League of Nations, they practiced diplomacy in what they considered to be the true bourgeois spirit—with as much disingenuousness, duplicity, and cynicism as they could get away with. Secretary of State Bainbridge Colby wrote indignantly in 1920 that the government of the United States had become convinced, against its will, that "the existing regime in Russia is based upon the negation of every principle of honor and good faith, and every usage and convention, underlying the whole structure of international law; the negation, in short, of every principle upon which it is possible to base harmonious and trustful relations, whether of nations or of individuals." How could there be any common ground, he asked, upon which the Western powers could stand with a government whose conceptions of international relations were so entirely alien to their own? This was a question that must often have been in the minds of diplomats whose governments could not, like the United States government, simply ignore the Soviet Union and who, therefore, had to go on trying to adjust their traditional concepts of diplomatic practice to Soviet wrecking tactics.

Nor did they have to concern themselves only with Lenin and his successors. Governments that resented the treatment they had received at Paris were not disinclined to follow the Soviet example, and some of them found leaders whose virtuosity matched that of the men sent forth from the Kremlin. Mussolini built a career upon his discovery that a flagrant breach of custom sometimes elicited more consternation than effective resistance; and Hitler won his early successes by means of outrageous falsehoods that were accepted by Western statesmen schooled in the tradition that diplomats were gentlemen and gentlemen did not lie to each other. In a sense, the whole period between the two world wars was a *dialogue des sourds* between those governments attempting to construct a genuine comity of nations on the ruins left by the war and seeking new rules that would be accepted by all its members, and those revolutionary powers that preferred to recognize no rules at all or desired to retain the freedom to determine when they would obey rules and when they would break them.

The degeneration of accepted standards of international intercourse and the confusion of the intellectual atmosphere in which diplomacy had to be conducted was further increased by the fact that the newly created or recently liberated nations were also likely to show a disinclination to accept traditional restraints. Their late arrival on the scene and their relative lack of status was often in itself a goad to defiance of the restrictions that a genuine community of nations requires; and in some cases resentments inherited from a colonial past inspired a rejection of legal arrangements, diplomatic principles, or methods of procedure simply because they were Western in origin or character. The behavior of the new nations—regarded from the standpoint of self-interest—was often illogical and self-defeating; but their leaders ignored this in their gratification over the confusion they proved capable of creating, and contributed powerfully to the complexities and the failures of communication of the new diplomacy.

Finally, it should be noted that in those countries having the greatest interest in maintaining public law and creating an effective international system after 1919, the ability of professional diplomats to cope with the problems caused by the war was seriously diminished by the loss of their former prestige and public support. In Great Britain and the United States in particular, it was widely believed that the diplomats had caused the war, because they had been the authors of what Woodrow Wilson called that "concatenation of alliances and treaties, [that] complicated network of intrigue and espionage which unerringly caught the entire family in its meshes." As if intent on sharing Lenin's prejudices, politicians in both countries demanded that foreign policy be removed from the hands of the professionals and turned over to the people and were roundly applauded for doing so. There was little objection (except among officials of the Foreign Office and the State Department) when heads of state began to use persons with no special qualification in foreign affairs as their diplomatic advisers, or to send politicians and businessmen abroad as envoys extraordinary in time of crisis, or even to go to foreign capitals themselves and to supersede their own ambassadors in negotiations.

George F. Kennan has written that summit diplomacy, a method of negotiation that has brought much imprecision and many unreasonable expectations into international intercourse since 1945, has its start during the Paris Peace Conference of 1919, where the Council of Four was a permanent summit conference in which heads of state, often without the assistance of professional diplomatic aides, sought to plaster loose formulae over intractable problems. Despite indifferent success at Paris, the experiment was carried further by the statesmen of the interwar period, the British being particularly prone to what came to be called "open diplomacy." Lloyd George, Ramsay MacDonald, and Neville Chamberlain all found it impossible to delegate the execution of policy and the delicate tasks of negotiation to professionals, of whom, indeed, they had an opinion bordering on contempt, and whose methods—the time-tested procedures of negotiation on the basis of written documents—they considered ill-suited to the conditions of the new age.

These tendencies, which had unfortunate results in British practice, were not confined to Britain. In France, when Briand and Laval were prime ministers, the Foreign Office was less than perfectly informed of the nature of their conversations with, and the extent of their commitments to, foreign statesmen like Stresemann and Mussolini. Nor would anyone deny that the distrust of professional diplomacy inspired by the First World War caused dislocation, imprecision, and confusion in the administration of foreign affairs in the United States. Wilson was not alone in his distrust of the techniques of the old diplomacy. The history of the London Economic Conference of 1933 and the elaborate methods employed subsequently by Franklin Roosevelt to by-pass the State Department (methods commented upon most recently in the memoirs of Robert Murphy) were in full accord with the kind of pattern set by the Council of Four in 1919 and Lloyd George's personal diplomacy in the years that followed.

III

In the middle of the nineteenth century, Sir Robert Peel defined diplomacy as the great machine whose primary purpose was the preservation of peace. The revolutionary impact of the First World War upon the size and homogeneity of the diplomatic community and upon the nature of diplomatic practice was admirably designed to make the fulfillment of that purpose impossible and to release once more the expanding energies of war upon the world. How could the newer and smaller powers learn to cultivate restraint, responsibility, and recognition of collective values when older and stronger powers so conspicuously lacked those qualities? How could the *velléités* of Ramsay MacDonald or the arrogant amateurishness of Neville Chamberlain cope with the brutal forthrightness and lack of scruple of Mussolini or the deliberate obstructionism of the Soviet Union? Or, for that matter, with the ambitions of Adolf Hitler, who regarded diplomacy not as a machine for peace but as a means of preparing the way for the destructive war after which he lusted?

The Second World War was, to a very large degree, the direct result of the revolution in diplomacy that had been set in motion in the years between 1914 and 1918. At the same time, the second global conflict demonstrated that the technological and psychological changes affecting warfare in 1914 could be raised to new and frightening dimensions. The war that begun with Stukas diving on Warsaw ended with the mushroom clouds over Hiroshima and Nagasaki, and, in the interval, any shadow of a line between soldier and civilian disappeared forever. The war became total to an extent that could not be exceeded; and it was fought with unimaginable bitterness to a point beyond all reason, until the destruction of the last vestiges of the system so badly shaken a quarter of a century before had been completed and the world had been handed over to the uncertainties of the Cold War.

The very employment of this term was an indication that war was threatening to become not only total but permanent, and that the passions that made men demand unconditional surrender in wartime were now affecting their minds as they thought about foreign policy in general. There were many occasions after the end of the Second World War when it appeared as if the democracies had won the war only to succumb to the views of diplomacy that had been professed by the totalitarian states. The whole atmosphere of international relations was impregnated with the smell of combat; and in the two great power centers of Washington and Moscow, the principal activity of diplomats seemed to be devoted to winning allies for some future, yet undisclosed, showdown. The idea of a compromise with the other side, of a *modus vivendi* that might stave off such a confrontation, seemed anathema to many people in the democracies; and Senator Joseph McCarthy found wide support when he conducted an investigation that soon became a persecution of supposedly unenthusiastic Cold Warriors in the diplomatic establishment. From being an instrument of policy, war seemed on the point of becoming its determinant.

And yet the very completeness of the technological revolution in warfare prevented these tendencies from reaching what might have seemed to be their logical conclusion. If, in a democratic age, where every man has a vital stake in foreign policy, war betrayed what Clausewitz once called a fatal thrust toward the absolute, it never quite got there. A sign that second thoughts might be asserting themselves was the fact that the Korean War was kept within bounds and restricted to the objectives that had been originally set for it, despite much violent talk about appeasement and about this being the only war the United States had ever lost. And in the subsequent period, diplomacy began to recover from the discredit that had been attached to it during the First World War and at periodic intervals thereafter, notably in the McCarthy episode. In the face of a clear possibility of a *dénouement* to the human drama like that portrayed in the film *Dr. Strangelove*, there grew a new appreciation of the uses of, and indeed a beginning of experimentation with new dimensions of, diplomacy.

In this last connection, we may revert to our starting point and recall the young idealists who dashed off to the front in 1914 with their hearts full of high resolve and their minds bent on that better world which would, they were sure, be the result of their sacrifice. It may be, as Professor Hermann Heimpel of the University of Cologne suggested in a recent address, that the present generation has rejected the notion that the highest good is to die for one's country and has substituted for this the ideal of living effectively for it instead. It may be that institutions like the Peace Corps—which has aroused so much interest and enthusiasm on American college campuses—may reveal new ways to achieve this ideal. In any event, it is permissible to hope that those members of the present generation who feel impelled, like Brooke's young men of 1914,

> *With hand made sure, clear eye, and sharpened power,*
> *To turn, as swimmers into cleanness leaping, . . .*

will turn, with all the idealism that is in them, to such works of mind and hand as may prevent the double revolution of war and diplomacy, to which these pages have been devoted, from reaching a fatal issue.

VI WITNESSES

We must restrict the number of witnesses that can be heard on the war's effects, lest this become a multivolume history of the past half century. Therefore, only three shall be quoted—one on the war's most momentous immediate effect, the Russian revolution; one on the peace the Allies wrote; and one on the most destructive of the long-range consequences of the war.

26 FROM *John Reed*

John Reed (1887–1920), American journalist, Communist activist, and friend of Lenin, like many Western intellectuals, was filled with high hopes as he watched the October revolution in Russia. This is the Moscow scene he describes as, early in November 1917, some of the dead are buried.

. . . Late in the night we went through the empty streets and under the Iberian gate to the great Red square in front of the Kremlin. The church of Basili Blazheini loomed fantastic, its bright-colored, convoluted and blazoned cupolas vague in the darkness. There was no sign of any damage. Along one side of the Square the dark towers and walls of the Kremlin stood up. On the high walls flickered redly the light of hidden flames; voices reached us across the immense place, and the sound of picks and shovels. We crossed over.

Mountains of dirt and rock were piled high near the base of the wall. Climbing these we looked down into two massive pits, ten or fifteen

SOURCE. John Reed, *Ten Days That Shook the World* (New York: Signet Books, 1967), pp. 225–229. Reprinted by permission of The New American Library.

feet deep and fifty yards long, where hundreds of soldiers and workers were digging in the light of huge fires.

A young student spoke to us in German. "The Brotherhood Grave," he explained. "To-morrow we shall bury here five hundred proletarians who died for the Revolution."

He took us down into the pit. In frantic haste swung the picks and shovels, and the earth-mountains grew. No one spoke. Overhead the night was thick with stars, and the ancient Imperial Kremlin wall towered up immeasurably.

"Here in this holy place," said the student, "holiest of all Russia, we shall bury our most holy. Here where are the tombs of the Tsars, our Tsar—the People—shall sleep. . . ."[1] His arm was in a sling, from a bullet-wound gained in the fighting. He looked at it. "You foreigners look down on us Russians because so long we tolerated a mediæval monarchy," said he. "But we saw that the Tsar was not the only tyrant in the world; capitalism was worse, and in all the countries of the world capitalism was Emperor. . . . Russian revolutionary tactics are best. . . ."

As we left, the workers in the pit, exhausted and running with sweat in spite of the cold, began to climb wearily out. Across the Red Square a dark knot of men came hurrying. They swarmed into the pits, picked up the tools and began digging, digging, without a word. . . .

So, all the long night volunteers of the People relieved each other, never halting in their driving speed, and the cold light of the dawn laid bare the great Square, white with snow, and the yawning brown pits of the Brotherhood Grave, quite finished.

We rose before sunrise, and hurried through the dark streets to Skobeliev Square. In all the great city not a human being could be seen; but there was a faint sound of stirring, far and near, like a deep wind coming. In the pale half-light a little group of men and women were gathered before the Soviet headquarters, with a sheaf of gold-lettered red banners—the Central Executive Committee of the Moscow Soviets. It grew light. From afar the vague stirring sound deepened and became louder, a steady and tremendous bass. The city was rising. We set out down the Tverskaya, the banners flapping overhead. The little street chapels along our way were locked and dark, as was the Chapel of the Iberian Virgin, which each new Tsar used to visit before he went to the Kremlin to crown himself, and which, day or night, was always open and crowded, and brilliant with

[1]Ellipses, here and throughout the text, are in the original. [Editor's note.]

the candles of the devout gleaming on the gold and silver and jewels of the ikons. Now, for the first time since Napoleon was in Moscow, they say, the candles were out.

The Holy Orthodox Church had withdrawn the light of its countenance from Moscow, the nest of irreverent vipers who had bombarded the Kremlin. Dark and silent and cold were the churches; the priests had disappeared. There were no popes to officiate at the Red Burial, there had been no sacrament for the dead, nor were any prayers to be said over the grave of the blasphemers. Tikhon, Metropolitan of Moscow, was soon to excommunicate the Soviets. . . .

Also the shops were closed, and the propertied classes stayed at home—but for other reasons. This was the Day of the People, the rumour of whose coming was thunderous as surf. . . .

Already through the Iberian Gate a human river was flowing, and the vast Red Square was spotted with people, thousands of them. I remarked that as the throng passed the Iberian Chapel, where always before the passerby had crossed himself, they did not seem to notice it. . . .

We forced our way through the dense mass packed near the Kremlin wall, and stood upon one of the dirt-mountains. Already several men were there, among them Muranov, the soldier who had been elected Commandant of Moscow—a tall, simple-looking, bearded man with a gentle face.

Through all the streets to the Red Square the torrents of people poured, thousands upon thousands of them, all with the look of the poor and the toiling. A military band came marching up, playing the *Internationale*, and spontaneously the song caught and spread like wind-ripples on a sea, slow and solemn. From the top of the Kremlin wall gigantic banners unrolled to the ground; red, with great letters in gold and in white, saying, "Martyrs of the Beginning of World Social Revolution," and "Long Live the Brotherhood of Workers of the World."

A bitter wind swept the Square, lifting the banners. Now from the far quarters of the city the workers of the different factories were arriving, with their dead. They could be seen coming through the Gate, the blare of their banners, and the dull red—like blood—of the coffins they carried. These were rude boxes, made of unplaned wood and daubed with crimson, borne high on the shoulders of rough men who marched with tears streaming down their faces, and followed by women who sobbed and screamed, or walked stiffly, with white, dead faces. Some of the coffins were open, the lid carried behind them;

others were covered with gilded or silvered cloth, or had a soldier's hat nailed on the top. There were many wreaths of hideous artificial flowers. . . .

Through an irregular lane that opened and closed again the procession slowly moved toward us. Now through the Gate was flowing an endless stream of banners, all shades of red, with silver and gold lettering, knots of crepe hanging from the top—and some Anarchist flags, black with white letters. The band was playing the Revolutionary Funeral March, and against the immense singing of the mass of people, standing uncovered, the paraders sang hoarsely, choked with sobs. . . .

Between the factory-workers came companies of soldiers with their coffins, too, and squadrons of cavalry, riding at salute, and artillery batteries, the cannon wound with red and black—forever, it seemed. Their banners said, "Long live the Third International!" or "We Want an Honest, General, Democratic Peace!"

Slowly the marchers came with their coffins to the entrance of the grave, and the bearers clambered up with their burdens and went down into the pit. Many of them were women—squat, strong proletarian women. Behind the dead came other women—women young and broken, or old, wrinkled women making noises like hurt animals, who tried to follow their sons and husbands into the Brotherhood Grave, and shrieked when compassionate hands restrained them. The poor love each other so!

All the long day the funeral procession passed, coming in by the Iberian Gate and leaving the Square by way of the Nikolskaya, a river of red banners, bearing words of hope and brotherhood and stupendous prophecies, against a background of fifty thousand people,—under the eyes of the world's workers and their descendants forever. . . .

One by one the five hundred coffins were laid in the pits. Dusk fell, and still the banners came drooping and fluttering, the band played the Funeral March, and the huge assemblage chanted. In the leafless branches of the trees above the grave the wreaths were hung, like strange, multi-coloured blossoms. Two hundred men began to shovel in the dirt. It rained dully down upon the coffins with a thudding sound, audible beneath the singing. . . .

The lights came out. The last banners passed, and the last moaning women, looking back with awful intensity as they went. Slowly from the great Square ebbed the proletarian tide. . . .

I suddenly realized that the devout Russian people no longer needed priests to pray them into heaven. On earth they were building a kingdom more bright than any heaven had to offer, and for which it was a glory to die. . . .

27 FROM *Harold Nicolson*

Two years later, greeted by some with equal optimism (did not the treaty provide for the creation of a League of Nations that would forever abolish the need for war?) came the Peace of Paris. In subsequent years, criticism of that treaty would become easy and universal. But at the time few, or at any rate few who like the losers were not engaged in special pleading, spoke out about its weaknesses. Among those who did was Harold Nicolson (1886–1968), then a junior member of the British delegation, who would go on to a distinguished career as a diplomat and author.

Printed first is a letter to his father, who had recently retired as British under-secretary of state for foreign affairs. It is followed by a description of the scene that took place on June 28, 1919, when the Germans signed the treaty. (It was a frequently repeated opinion of Nicolson's that—given the Allies' probable reluctance to resume the war—the Germans should have taken a tougher stand and refused their signature.)

JUNE 8, SUNDAY

I have every hope that Lloyd George, who is fighting like a Welsh terrier, will succeed in the face of everybody in introducing some modification in the terms imposed upon Germany. Now that we see them as a whole we realise that they are much too stiff. They are not stern merely but actually *punitive*, and they abound with what Smuts calls "pin pricks" as well as dagger thrusts. Lloyd George is concentrating upon Silesia, the cost of the Armies of Occupation, and the admission of Germany into the League of Nations. Yet the real crime is the reparation and indemnity chapter, which is immoral and senseless. There is not a single person among the younger people here who is not unhappy and disappointed at the terms. The only people who approve are the old fire-eaters. I have tried, with the help of the

SOURCE. Harold Nicolson, *Peacemaking 1919* (New York: The Universal Library, Grosset & Dunlap, 1965), pp. 359, 367–369. Reprinted by permission of Harcourt, Brace Jovanovich, Inc.

Treasury man, who is first class, to water down the Austrian financial clauses, but was told by Sumner to mind my own business. Anyhow I think we shall, provided Ll. G. wins his battle, get the Germans to sign. God help us if we can't! They will have us at their mercy.

JUNE 28, SATURDAY

. . . People step over the Aubusson benches and escabeaux to talk to friends. Meanwhile the delegates arrive in little bunches and push up the central aisle slowly. Wilson and Lloyd George are among the last. They take their seats at the central table. The table is at last full. Clemenceau glances to right and left. People sit down upon their escabeaux but continue chattering. Clemenceau makes a sign to the ushers. They say "Ssh! Ssh! Ssh!" People cease chattering and there is only the sound of occasional coughing and the dry rustle of programmes. The officials of the Protocol of the Foreign Office move up the aisle and say, "Ssh! Ssh!" again. There is then an absolute hush, followed by a sharp military order. The Gardes Républicains at the doorway flash their swords into their scabbards with a loud click. "Faites entrer les Allemands," says Clemenceau in the ensuing silence. His voice is distant but harshly penetrating. A hush follows.

Through the door at the end appear two huissiers with silver chains. They march in single file. After them come four officers of France, Great Britain, America and Italy. And then, isolated and pitiable, come the two German delegates. Dr. Müller, Dr. Bell. The silence is terrifying. Their feet upon a strip of parquet between the savonnerie carpets echo hollow and duplicate. They keep their eyes fixed away from those two thousand staring eyes, fixed upon the ceiling. They are deathly pale. They do not appear as representatives of a brutal militarism. The one is thin and pink-eyelidded: the second fiddle in a Brunswick orchestra. The other is moon-faced and suffering: a privatdozent. It is all most painful.

They are conducted to their chairs. Clemenceau at once breaks the silence. "Messieurs," he rasps, "la séance est ouverte." He adds a few ill-chosen words. "We are here to sign a Treaty of Peace." The Germans leap up anxiously when he has finished, since they know that they are the first to sign. William Martin, as if a theater manager, motions them petulantly to sit down again. Mantoux translates Clemenceau's words into English. Then St. Quentin advances towards the Germans and with the utmost dignity leads them to the little table on which the Treaty is expanded. There is general tension. They sign. There is a general relaxation. Conversation hums again in an undertone. The delegates stand up one by one and pass onwards to the queue which waits by the signature table. Meanwhile people buzz round the main table getting autographs. The single file of plenipotentiaries waiting to approach the table gets thicker. It goes quickly. The officials of the Quai d'Orsay stand round, indicating places to sign, indicating procedure, blotting with neat little pads.

Suddenly from outside comes the crash of guns thundering a salute. It announces to Paris that the second Treaty of Versailles has been signed by Dr. Müller and Dr. Bell. Through the few open windows comes the sound of distant crowds cheering hoarsely. And still the signature goes on.

We had been warned it might last three hours. Yet almost at once it seemed that the queue was getting thin. Only three, then two, and then one delegate remained to sign. His name had hardly been blotted before the huissiers began again their "Ssh! Ssh!" cutting suddenly short the wide murmur which had again begun. There was a final hush. "La séance est levée" rasped Clemenceau. Not a word more or less.

We kept our seats while the Germans were conducted like prisoners from the dock, their eyes still fixed upon some distant point of the horizon. . . .

28 FROM *Adolf Hitler*

Defeat and revolution in Russia, defeat and revolution in Austria, defeat and revolution in Germany. Among those whose lives were affected by the great European upheaval was a twenty-nine-year-old corporal in a Bavarian infantry regiment, who was recovering, in a hospital behind the lines, from wounds he had received at the Western front. When news of the German collapse reached him, it blended with certain earlier fixed ideas of his, to culminate in a resolve that he here describes.

. . . On November 10, the pastor came to the hospital for a brief speech. Now we learned everything.

SOURCE. Adolf Hitler, *Mein Kampf* (Munich: Verlag Franz Eher, 1930), pp. 222–225.

It was in a state of extreme agitation that I joined his audience. The dignified old gentleman seemed to be shaking when he told us that the House of Hohenzollern was no longer allowed to wear the German imperial crown; that our fatherland had become a "republic;" that we must pray to the Almighty not to refuse his blessing to this change and not to abandon our nation in the times to come. He could not help himself—he had to speak a few words in honor of the royal house. He meant to appreciate what it had done, for Pomerania, for Prussia, nay, for the German fatherland, when he began to weep softly to himself. Every heart, I think, was heavy with sorrow in that little hall, and not an eye that could hold back the tears. But when the old gentleman tried to go on, and began to tell us that we must now make an end to the long war, that having lost it and being at the mercy of the victors the fatherland was facing terrible times, but that trusting in the generosity of our former enemies we should accept the armistice—when he said that I could stand it no longer. I could not remain for another moment. Things went black before my eyes again, and on unsteady feet I groped my way back to the dormitory. I threw myself on my bunk, and buried my burning head into my blanket and pillow.

I had not wept since that day when I stood by my mother's grave. When, in my youth, fate dealt harshly with me, that just added to my spirit of defiance. When, in the long years of the war, death fetched a good comrade and friend from our ranks, it would have seemed all but a sin to me to complain—for they were dying for Germany! When, in the last days of the frightful struggle, the creeping gas attacked me and began to gnaw at my eyes, and fearful of going permanently blind I nearly lost heart for a moment, the voice of my conscience thundered at me: Miserable wretch! You cry while thousands are a hundred times worse off than you? And so I bore my lot in dull silence. But now I could not help myself. Only now did I see how all personal suffering is as nothing compared with the misfortunes of the fatherland.

It had all been in vain, then. In vain the sacrifices and the privations, in vain the hunger and the thirst of sometimes endless months, in vain the hours when, gripped though we were by mortal fear, we did our duty nonetheless, and in vain the death of the two million who gave their lives in the midst of these sufferings. . . .

There followed terrible days and even worse nights. I knew that all was lost. Only fools could place their hope in the enemies' mercy, fools—or liars and criminals. During these nights, my hatred grew, hatred for those responsible for this deed.

In the days that followed, I became aware of what my fate was to be. I had to laugh now when I cast my mind back to my thoughts about my future, which only very recently had so greatly worried me. Why, it was laughable to expect to build a house on such foundations. At last it became clear to me that what had happened was something that I had often feared, but that my emotions had prevented me from believing.

Kaiser Wilhelm II had been the first German emperor to proffer the hand of friendship to the Marxists, without suspecting that villains have no honor. While they still held the emperor's hand in theirs, their other hand was reaching for the dagger.

You cannot make a pact with Jews. All you can offer them is a harsh either-or.

I, for my part, decided to go into politics.

EPILOGUE

There is no call for cheers
There'll be no triumph
Instead
Worlds that you knew will die
And without dignity

STEFAN GEORGE, *Der Krieg* (1917)

The First World War failed to produce Utopia, resembling in this every human endeavor since the beginning of time.

A. J. P. TAYLOR, *Illustrated History of the First World War*

. . . It is easy enough for us today, who have long since struck the word "security" from our vocabulary, to smile at the optimistic delusions of a generation that wore the blinders of idealism, a generation that believed that mankind's technological progress must of necessity lead to an equally rapid moral improvement. We have become more skeptical about the possibilities for the ethical advance of the human species. The new century has taught us, after all, not to be surprised by any outbreak of collective bestiality. . . . We have, as far as our own lives are concerned, long ago abandoned the religion of our fathers, that is their faith in a quick and lasting progress of the human kind. We remember our cruel lessons, and find that their rash optimism strikes us as banal. For we live in an age where a single catastrophe has undone a thousand years of human effort.

SOURCE. Stefen Zweig, *Die Welt von Gestern* (Frankfurt: S. Fischer Verlag, 1947), pp. 19–20.

Yet, even though it may have been a delusion our fathers served, it was a splendid and noble delusion, more constructive and humane than the slogans of today. And there is something in me that keeps me from entirely abandoning it, despite all that I have come to understand recently. That which, in his childhood, a man has absorbed into his bloodstream from the very air around him cannot be taken from him. So, in spite of everything that daily assault my ears, in spite of all the humiliations and all the trials that I and the many who share my fate have experienced, I cannot wholly deny the faith of my youth—that some day things will move forward again, in spite of everything, yes in spite of everything. Even in the abyss of despair in which, half blind, we grope about today, our souls distorted or broken, I again and again look up to the ancient lodestars that shone over my childhood, and comfort myself with the inherited confidence that this terrible relapse will appear, in days to come, as a mere interval in the eternal rythm of the onward and onward. . . .

NOTE ON FURTHER READING

To add a detailed bibliography to this book would seem pretentious. It also would be unnecessary, since many such bibliographies already are available, including several recent ones. The reader interested in pursuing the topics dealt with in this volume is referred to the bibliographies in the following books: For the causes of the war, Luigi Albertini, *The Origins of the War of 1914* and Joachim Remak, *The Origins of World War I*; for the war's conduct, Hanson W. Baldwin, *World War I* and Correlli Barnett, *The Swordbearers*; and for the aftermath, René Albrecht-Carrié, *The Meaning of the First World War* and Arno J. Mayer, *Politics and Diplomacy of Peacemaking*.

Since readers may also want a better look at the books from which excerpts have been printed here, this is a fitting-place to express the editor's appreciation to a number of publishers for their generous permission to reprint copyrighted material. Full bibliographical details were given with each selection, and there is no need to repeat these here, but what is worth reiterating is that without the kind cooperation of the author and publishers cited, this book could not exist.

There remains one other source of help to be noted. It is that given by three people at the University of California at Santa Barbara, by Alan Beyerchen, Bruce Loynd, and Robert Young. The facts and ideas that they contributed have made this a far better volume than the editor, unaided, could have presented.